Take One

TAKE • ONE

Television Directors
on
Directing

JACK KUNEY

PRAEGER

New York
Westport, Connecticut
London

Library of Congress Cataloging-in-Publication Data

Kuney, Jack.
    Take one : television directors on directing / Jack
Kuney.
        p.   cm.
    Includes bibliographical references.
    ISBN 0-275-93546-9 (pbk. : alk. paper)
    1. Television—Production and direction.   2. Television producers
and directors—Interviews.   I. Title.
    [PN1992.75.K86 1990b]
    791.45'0233'0922—dc20   89-72126

Copyright © 1990 by Jack Kuney

A hardcover edition of *Take One* is available from
Greenwood Press (Contributions to the Study of Popular
Culture; 25; ISBN 0-313-26384-1).

Library of Congress Catalog Card Number: 89-72126
ISBN: 0-275-93546-9

First published in 1990

Praeger Publishers, One Madison Avenue, New York, NY 10010
A division of Greenwood Press, Inc.

Printed in the United States of America

The paper used in this book complies with the
Permanent Paper Standard issued by the National
Information Standards Organization (Z39.48–1984).

10   9   8   7   6   5   4   3   2   1

I can't tell you how many times, in the panic of the control room, I have turned to my technical director, and shouted, "TAKE ONE!" and then have him turn to me and say, "George, you're already on *one*."

George Paul

☆
_____

Contents

☆

Introduction

An aura of mystery surrounds the television director as he enters his personal domain—the control room. The room is slightly darkened, filled with electronic state-of-the-art equipment—dimmed so that multiple monitors carrying pictures from studios, newsrooms, auditoriums, stages and playing fields of varying sizes and shapes can convey their images from several different angles, piercing the blackness with clarity and conviction, allowing the director dominion over all he sees.

Dressed informally, concentrating intensely, the director goes about his work in this half-light, signaling to a technician alongside him which monitor he wants to bring on line. Some do it by a nod of the head, some by snapping fingers aggressively, others by a pencil tap on the script. Some, in situations of less magnitude, accomplish their task by pushing buttons on the control panel—the switcher—themselves.

What the director is doing as he selects his shots is determining what millions of viewers will be seeing on TV sets in their homes. In the case of the nightly news, a sporting event, an occasional special happening, a rare concert or opera, the director's decision affects viewers instantly; in the case of most other programming, he is circumscribing what will be videotaped, preparing program content for shows that are stockpiled and broadcast at a later date.

Average television viewers are totally unaware of this directorial thrust and have little or no interest in what goes on behind the camera, unless it has to do with the personalities that people their television screen. Even when something goes terribly wrong with their picture, viewers are more likely to blame the manufacturer of the set, their own technical incompetence or the cable system they buy, rather than the people who are producing the program.

In truth, for average viewers, it really isn't that important that they recognize the contribution that a director makes to a television program. But for the thousands of students in this country who some day hope to make their livelihood in the world of television and for the thousands of aspiring young directors who work for stations and networks across the country, it's crucial to recognize that role and even more, the truth that some people are better than others at it— directing.

As viewers, we recognize only whether the show has succeeded or failed, and we usually indicate that displeasure by tuning out, by twisting the dial. Individual accomplishment by people who create programs matters little. Occasionally a video artist gains stature in the eye of the public, but that person is usually a writer or a producer of an extraordinarily popular situation comedy, game show or suspense-adventure drama.

As in great theatre, it is sometimes difficult to sort out and recognize the accomplishments of each individual who made the play or, in this case, the program work. We do not recognize the contributions of the individuals involved: the fine hand of the director, the designer, the lighting director, let alone the talent of the actors. We acknowledge only the success or failure of the production.

One writer suggests that the only person deserving of recognition in television is the producer, noting that TV is a "producer's medium" and further suggesting that the "producer is the audience until the audience sees the show."[1] Needless to say, that author is a producer himself.

In television, the director's contribution is often cloistered, hidden in the darkness of his control room. This wasn't so from the beginning. Television really took off, began its extraordinary, almost exponential, growth in 1948. And in those early days, television directors came from two pools of talent: the theatre and film. A few technical people were willing to try, but they were scorned as being "techies," people without artistry. In the so-called "Golden Age"[2] of television, the cynics were proved wrong. Out of the control room came a whole group of talented men who had technical mastery of the medium as well as the ability to stage and shoot a play with great skill—men with style as well as substance. Among the names we still remember from the Golden Age are Sidney Lumet, Frank Schaffner, Ralph Nelson, John Frankenheimer, George Roy Hill and Delbert Mann. It's interesting to note that most of these men turned their back on television, deciding instead to follow careers in the making of feature films.

What gave the Golden Age its roseate hue was the production of fine drama, uniquely designed for the small screen. In this era of creative production, there were splendid producers who were men of vision, like David Susskind and Fred Coe, but it became the director's job to turn that vision into reality, to make those closet dramas the wonder that they were. Through careful planning, intensive rehearsal and long studio days, the directors of the Golden Age learned their craft, but even more, because they were men of intelligence and perception, they quickly learned the value of their aesthetic decisions.

How can the director's contribution be identified? Minimally, the director determines what the viewers see, how closely they see it and in what sequence they see it. But is there more to the process than this?

This book will affirm that there is more—much more. In a series of ten interviews with directors of television programs, each a specialist in a different field, this text unravels some of the mystery of that control room conundrum. It makes a case for the director, showing that more often than not it is the director, with his instincts and well-honed talent, who sets the tone of the program and goes a long way toward determining what impact that show will have on its audience. Hopefully, this is accomplished without denigrating in any way the functions of the other two members of the production triumvirate responsible for a program, the writer and the producer.

The basis for these conclusions will be the words of the directors themselves. The interviews that follow were collected over a period of four years. Some of them (with Kirk Browning, Sandy Grossman and George Schaefer) have appeared in *Television Quarterly,* the publication of the National Academy of the Television Arts and Sciences. These directors show incredible diversity, going from Hollywood to New York with ease, focusing equally on cultural institutions like the Metropolitan Opera and bastions of gamesmanship like the Super Bowl.

I also wish to thank Herman Land, who serves as chairman of the *Quarterly*'s editorial board, and Richard Pack, its editor, for their valuable support and encouragement. Thanks are also due to the faculty and students of the Brooklyn College Department of Television and Radio and to its chairman, Robert C. Williams, all of whom helped to turn my thirty years of television production experience into a teaching adventure.

In explaining the role of the director, I must underscore the obvious fact that television programs differ, and so does the degree of the director's involvement. Although it may appear otherwise at times, in making TV shows, we don't turn out the equivalent of cars on an assembly line. Each program is an entity of and by itself, and the director's role changes with the nature of the program.

But no matter the program, there is always a director working, organizing content, selecting and shaping the material, meeting deadlines. From the sitcoms of Hollywood and the soap operas of New York to the *Movie of the Week* and the plays of public television, there is always a director in command. The sites and scenes where directors function are endless: athletic contests, pageants and parades (everything from football to Ping-Pong, from Miss America to body building), concerts, operas, variety shows, game shows, news, documentaries, discussions, special events, dance programs, panel shows—the list goes on. Through it all, the director moves silently and efficiently.

Each show is different, and a predilection for the material is usually advisable, but not mandated. Directors take on the strangest assignments without thought of failure, assuming that they can fill the gaps in their background without difficulty, becoming instant experts. The classic case in point is that of Orson Welles. The young genius, flushed with his success at the Mercury Theatre, was offered his first movie, *Citizen Kane,* and moved impudently into the director's chair, stopping only on the way to enlist the support of a great cameraman, Greg Toland. The rest is history. Knowing almost nothing about movie making, he went on to make a great movie. He was an exception. The fact is that the more a director knows, the better he is able to guide the talented technicians that he works with. Welles knew his own technical limitations and enlisted the support of his crew, secure in his aesthetic judgments.

It's a paradox, for television programs differ, just as the personalities who direct them do. Some shows take months of pre-preparation by the director, weeks to shoot. In Hollywood, with the need to keep feeding the money machine, directors move into sitcoms on the week of shooting. Involving themselves with little more than the movement of already set situations, they become magicians, squeezing time into unbelievable and new conformations.

On film, the director's skills are canonized. The French refer to their film makers as "auteurs," the authors of cinema. Conversely, Bob Shanks[3] eulogizes his fellow producers as "the only audience," completely ignoring the director and his contribution. Somewhere in between lies the truth, and this is what is explored in this text. Most of the conclusions drawn will emerge from the director's own words, with the author's commentary acting as a guide and summation. Each talented director interviewed had something very different and very relevant to say, and that's the key to the book. The director's eye is the antecedent of the camera's eye, and each sees things differently. The subjects we have chosen are certainly not the only talented directors in the field, for there are lots of talented people around although, unfortunately, as in many fields, the gifted are outnumbered by those who are less talented. But the insights of the people we interviewed are extraordinary, and what emerges from the conversations is the nature of their unique contributions: what goes on behind the camera to bring something into being, to establish its reality; what conceptually sets the program, brings it into focus; what allows its images to emerge with clarity and truth.

Finally, I might add that after thirty years on location and in studios making TV shows and guiding other people in their efforts to make them, it was my unique experience to become a full-time teacher, passing on some of the things that I had learned in my long career. My job was twofold: teaching a full schedule of production and writing courses and coordinating the Master of Fine Arts program at Brooklyn College. It was endlessly fascinating for me, as I began to re-examine some of the skills and techniques that I had come to depend on as a producer, a director, and a writer, learning as I did, late in life, ways in which I could teach those skills in the classroom.

There were many fine textbooks to draw upon—Zettl, Bretz, Millerson, Burroughs and Wood—but in most cases, there just wasn't adequate space or time in those texts to get beyond the description of equipment and the basics of shooting style. Almost none dealt with the aesthetics of television. One book that I felt did try to set a series of principles for communicating visually on television was Colby Lewis's *The TV Director/Interpreter*.

Many books on film and theatre deal with aesthetic judgments, but in television they are rare, which may in some small way be a commentary on the medium. Lewis's stated wish was "to convey to the audience the right sights and the right sounds at the right times. . . . "[4] Over twenty years old, the book does try to expand the concepts behind most of the decisions that a TV director has to make. I have used the book successfully in most of my advanced directing classes. Unfortunately, no revised edition is planned, and the book shows its age.

But I thought of Lewis as I started to conduct the interviews that are the basis of this book, hearing in the answers to my questions some of his succinct and simple insights. I still did not have a textbook in mind as I proceeded through four years of interviews, but as I now sift through this archive, I cannot help but think how valuable some of this intelligence would be to a student of production who hopes to cross over the fine line between the classroom and the studios and sites where he will exercise his professional skills, or to an aspiring young director moving from his role as a stage manager or an assistant into the director's chair.

If you discern a predilection for describing most of the characters in this text in the male gender, please understand that no sexual slight is intended. In spite of a concerted push by the almost 7,000 members of the Director's Guild of America to bring more women into its ranks, less than 2 percent of the membership of the Guild are women, and less than 1 percent work in some sort of supervisory directorial position. This picture is slowly improving and hopefully will continue to do so in the ensuing years.

NOTES

1. Bob Shanks, *The Cool Fire: How to Make It in Television* (New York: W. W. Norton, 1976).

2. Max Wilk, *The Golden Age of Television* (New York: Delacorte Press, 1976).

3. Shanks, *The Cool Fire.*

4. Colby Lewis, *The TV Director/Interpreter* (New York: Hastings House, 1968).

Take One

Kirk Browning

Kirk Browning: Directing at the Metropolitan Opera House

Kirk Browning does not describe himself as a musician, but he says that he is *musical*. He attributes about 80 percent of whatever he has been able to achieve in television—the programs and the plays, as well as the concerts and the opera—to that musicality.

I think that any director, basically, has to be musical. George Roy Hill is the most musical director I know, and he does almost no musical shows. But there's music in everything that he touches. And I'm very fortunate to have been born very musical. I have a response to music. I feel textures and rhythms and dynamics—whatever strength I have as a director comes out of those—out of that sense of direction.

I talked with Kirk over a period of two days in his apartment overlooking Central Park West in New York City. Watching the joggers cut through the park, I was reminded that Kirk, too, was a jogger, even though he was in his sixties, and religiously did his early morning six-mile run.

A tall, fine-looking man, Kirk is one of the most remarkable people you will ever meet. With his boyish frame, topped by a shock of white hair, he exudes good health, has tremendous energy and generates warmth and camaraderie to a degree that's almost embarrassing. A casual greeting from Kirk on a street corner in Manhattan is like a reunion with a long lost brother or sister, unseen for twenty years.

Portions of this chapter appeared previously in *Television Quarterly,* a publication of the Academy of Television Arts and Sciences, vol. 20, no. 4, 1984.

It's a wonderful trait in a director, and wherever he goes, Kirk leaves a loving trail of friends and associates behind him. It was one of those early friends, Samuel Chotzinoff, the musical director for the National Broadcasting Company in the late forties, who convinced Kirk to join NBC in 1947 and work in the music library. These were exciting days for music at the network. The NBC Symphony, a virtuoso orchestra under the baton of Maestro Arturo Toscanini, was giving weekly radio concerts with televised simulcasts in the offing, and plans for a weekly live opera on television were being discussed.

Kirk became a stage manager in 1948 on that first opera, Kurt Weill's *Down in the Valley*. By 1950, Kirk was directing his first opera, a one-act opera by Offenbach entitled *Monsieur Choufleury*. At about the same time, he started directing the telecasts of the NBC Symphony.

Did I ever tell you how I got to be the director of the NBC Symphony concerts with Toscanini? They had a sports director doing them because it was a remote, out of studio, in Carnegie Hall. He'd read on the program that one of the selections was going to be "The Girl with the Flaxen Hair" by Debussy. At the time I was working with Chotzinoff. I don't think I was any more than an [assistant director] at the time, but anyhow, I was watching the program on a monitor at Carnegie Hall with Chotzy as it was going on live. I'm looking at a picture of the maestro, Toscanini, conducting, and all of a sudden, supered over the maestro's face, is this picture of a girl sitting in front of a mirrored lily pond combing her hair with a brush!

Chotzy turned to me and he said, "Kirk, from here on, you're directing the Toscanini shows. I don't care what you do with the picture—just never be on anything but Toscanini."

So that's how I started doing the NBC Symphony!

A career in television as a result of a needless superimposition! I asked Kirk, rather facetiously, if he ever got a chance to shoot the musicians after Chotzinoff's admonition.

Not without Toscanini in the picture. There was never a single shot that didn't include Toscanini in it.

The first think that I did was to move all my cameras behind the orchestra. In those days, you didn't have zoom lenses, so the only way I could get various pictures of the maestro, without his back, was to move everything around.

That really started the whole technique of shooting the reverse angle.

In Europe, they're still shooting TV concerts the way an audience sees them—selections of the orchestra and the conductor from the side or the back. But the whole idea of shooting over instruments into the conductor was something unique.

Kirk went on to tell me that he had recently seen a kinescope of one of those early Toscanini simulcasts at the Museum of Broadcasting in New York City, and he indicated that he wouldn't change a thing if he were preparing the orchestra for the broadcast today. He told me that the miracle of the whole thing was that the director was literally forced into a successful shooting style.

You couldn't move the camera, and you had to have enormously long takes. Today, I just cut and move. I never stand still. But the maestro was one of those extraordinary people. The more you stayed on him, the better the picture.

A simply discovery, but a very basic one—the power of the unadorned picture. Marshall McLuhan, television's only recognizable philosopher, once noted that the ideal television image consisted of one person on a screen being watched by one person in a home. The symbiosis is perfect. (And it is why our anchors on the nightly news become larger than life.)

In this day and age of heightened expectations, we watch *Miami Vice,* MTV, a mixed bag of rock concerts and the new soft-focus, back-lit, quick-cut commercials that are so disruptive of program content, and we have a tendency as viewer/directors to ignore the simple truth behind McLuhan's simple observation. If a single shot has any power at all, that power does not diminish as the shot sustains; it only increases. Hence, as Colby Lewis tells us: "Don't cut just for the sake of cutting, cut only when you cut to a better shot."*

The directors of the Golden Age of television were forced into a simpler shooting style because of the size and the complexity of the early cameras—they were about six feet long from the tip of the lens to the eyepiece of the cameraman. The pedestals of those early cameras weighed anywhere from four to six hundred pounds; the camera itself weighed two to three hundred. There were no zoom lenses; the camera had a turret up front with four separate lenses attached. These had to be physically adjusted by the cameraman

*Colby Lewis, *The TV Director/Interpreter* (New York: Hastings House, 1968).

from behind the camera, under instructions from the director in the control room or on the studio floor. Directors blocked with extreme care, spending long days and nights before their shows plotting each shot in their script, working with a template that measured the angles and lengths of their four different lenses, charting their shots on a studio floor plan, carefully marking their scripts. They knew and recognized the value of each shot, mainly because each was so damned difficult to achieve.

With featherweight cameras, zoom lenses, and automatic focus, we move quicker and with greater ease in the studio and on location, but I fear with much less accuracy. The experiences of those early directors should not be forgotten. I asked Kirk Browning just how precise he was when it came to planning his shoots.

It depends on the degree of control I have. If I cover an opera at the Met, most of my work has already been done for me. All I have to do is photograph the performance. Now, obviously, I'm trying to do several things in reporting the whole business with my cameras. I'm attempting to let the TV audience see what the live audience is seeing, so that they have some feeling of sharing something—a common language.

My main interest is people. I think one of the strengths of working out of some place like the Metropolitan Opera House is that you are able to exhibit—put right up front—Pavarotti and Domingo and Sutherland. There may be twenty other people doing something interesting on the stage, but if there's a Pavarotti or a Sutherland or a Domingo, I'll find some way of keeping the reference on them almost the entire time—simply because that's what the audience is interested in.

It seemed extraordinary for a director to lock one camera in on one character in an opera, so I questioned his tactic.

When the Met is doing a production featuring one of their great superstars like Luciano Pavarotti, I will anchor a camera, in terms of emphasis, picture and action, on that star. I will design my shoot so that person is related to almost everything that is happening on stage. Now, it isn't always possible because the person is standing there with his back turned, not doing anything—then you just forget it, get on with the rest of your show.

I'm convinced that you can't be hidebound as a director; you have to be flexible. Time is always of the essence in television. I have never seen a TV situation in which you can lie back and relax—decisions must be made quickly and alertly in the studio and on location, and as Kirk says, if something isn't working, "get on with the rest of your show."

Kirk then went on to explain his physical setup at the Met, using six cameras. Aspiring directors are always intimidated by large numbers of cameras on a shoot, with subsequent multiple monitors in the control room. The logistics of a shoot of an Oscar night, or the Rose Bowl Parade or the Super Bowl seem so complex that in their wildest imagination student directors cannot make the transition from the two or three cameras they are using in studio practice. I try to reassure them, saying that the same principles apply whether it's two cameras or twenty.

One of your main objectives as a director is to avoid distortion, and one of the ways of achieving this is to avoid extremes of height or depth or width. Most directors work their cameras at the eye level of the performer. This is just as true in a drama or the nightly news as it is for Kirk in the presentation of opera.

Shooting a show from the audience always poses problems in trying to achieve eye level. Auditoriums dip or rise precipitously, and placing the camera on a platform or in a tunnel leading to the auditorium is sometimes mandated in order to maintain eye level. Each location is different and must be observed for those differences; then, once again, we can go back to our basic shooting principles. Kirk continued:

At the Met, I usually put two cameras at the extreme ends of the orchestra pit, both on the left side and the right side of the conductor, almost lower than stage level. I try not to impinge on the audience's sightlines; after all, we can't clear the audience out. But they're at a very low angle— as low as I can get them and still see the stage. That gives me four cameras across the front, and I have two more cameras rather far back and a bit higher up on the side boxes. I don't use the center box ordinarily, unless I am working with Franco Zeffirelli. When I did *La Boheme* for Zeffirelli, he said, "Kirk, you can do anything you want, but please give me a center shot of the set—it's the one thing I want." So I gave it to him. I just put a camera in the center box, simply to show him each of the sets head-on. But ordinarily I don't bother to do that . . . that's not what the audience is really going to remember.

We continued our discussion of shooting style, concentrating now on his use of those cameras that he had placed at the extreme ends of the orchestra—cross-shooting. Here, Kirk surprised me a bit because I always tell my students (once again, for clarity's sake) to concentrate on the full-front face, if possible, in their shooting. Like any creative person, Kirk had his variations.

I know it must sound heretical, but I found that the most interesting and theatrical way to shoot grand opera singers is off the full face, from the side and rather low. They seem to retain their kind of larger-than-life persona that way. I don't go for the high shot that a lot of the European opera houses use—the box that shows a lot of floor, and the singers, from overhead . . . I've always thought it was demeaning to the performer. It just makes him look unimportant, uninteresting.

Most good directors have a shooting style that is recognizable, and that is certainly true in Kirk's case. One of the hallmarks of his work is a camera that is constantly in motion: constantly zooming in, constantly zooming out. I asked him about this.

I think I do a little too much, but if I'm going to err on any side, I'm going to err on the side of what I would call an active camera. In a way, you see, it's as though the camera were a committed member of the audience. It gives you a point of view about what's going on. If you sit too long on a frozen shot, with the camera totally passive, what you're doing stops being subjective. I'm trying to use a subjective camera in the sense that the camera is one person exploring everything. And when you explore, you are active; you don't just sit there.

The thing about television is, if you think of it as a set of eyes looking at a piece of material, and somehow transmitted to an audience, the director's psyche is such that he can see a wide shot or a close-up, a medium shot, or he can pan. He can do all these things, individually, yet there's a continual psychic activity. You know your involvement in what is going on ahead of you. What you do is always in the context of an overall framework, so that you don't really think of each shot as being an interrupted series of impressions.

One thing that occurred to me as we were talking was that audiences don't watch television to watch cameras at work. The audience wants to be involved in the program, whatever its nature. And if they are not involved, they will tune you out sooner than you can say "Walter Cronkite."

That's the paradox of our business. It would appear as though it's simply self-aggrandizement on the director's part to assume all those judgments about when you should be close and when you should be far. Well the point is that if you're clever enough about it, it should look like the judgment of the home viewer. It should look as though it's what the home viewer needs to see, and it's not the director being gratuitous.

You can't possibly please every viewer because they each come with different perceptions. If I were doing an orchestra show for a convention of timpani players, obviously they would want to see what the timpani is doing. So, if I know that, I'd probably structure the show so that 80 percent of the time I am on the timpani. There's no easy answer as to how you treat these things. I'm basically trying to appeal to a lay audience who has no particular predisposition for any one aspect of this. They simply want an experience which is not going to bore them, and so I do what I think the general audience will respond to.

At this point, our conversation turned to one aspect of television that had always given me pause: the efficacy of where you produce things, where you locate your shows, how things look, the power that a director has, if any, when working with a scenic designer or is a designer himself. I have always been surprised to note how many successful designers move on to become even more successful producers and directors in film and television—Franco Zeffirelli, for example. Less known, perhaps, but equally as successful in making the transition to TV production and direction are such people as Herb Brodkin, Marvin Chomsky and Gary Smith—designers all.

How you see something is often more important than just the mere act of reportage. There are so many bad plays (mainly on cable television or on PBS) where the production suffered only because of the unwillingness or inability of the producer/director to move his cameras on stage where they could reflect on what was going on in the play, present a point of view.

Imposing television's limitations on a staged performance of an opera can often help that performance—most opera is so grandiose that TV can cut it down to manageable size—but shooting a play off the stage can often be a disaster. When you are working under a proscenium arch, and trying to use a TV camera, especially from center stage, you have eliminated more than 50 percent of that stage, unless you have decided to stay wide all the time, eliminating tight shots, reaction shots and detail. Someone once described the television picture from your average camera as covering "the short end of a funnel," and, as a consequence, when you examine the stage that remains, you might note that you have eliminated all that once was downstage left and right.

It's one of the reasons that Kirk depends so heavily on the pairs of cameras that he has on each side of the orchestra—it's the only way that he can approximate any action that looks at all reasonable in his operas. He uses his cameras at the back of the house only for long zooms and tight shots of his stars. Kirk went on:

You have so many opportunities on television that you don't have on the proscenium stage; a director's just missing the boat if he thinks literally in stage terms. Of course, a lot depends on the amount of money that you have been given. But in the case of opera, unless you're a great artist like a Zeffirelli or a Ponelle,* you should not go out and shoot on location. There's something about a totally realistic environment that seems so silly when people are singing opera. Ponelle and Zeffirelli are great enough artists, so that they take a realistic setting and make it theatrical, they make it a metaphor for something. . . . Their eye is so right they know how to make a meadowland look like something besides a meadowland when someone comes out and sings in it.

Kirk ranks very highly among the working directors in New York City who have a finely applied aesthetic sense. Not that he consciously makes pretty pictures as he directs, although they are generally pleasing. Kirk is just not able to function any differently than he does, considering his psychological and social makeup. Here, for example, he reflects on the difficulty of achieving unique shots and tells the story behind one important aesthetic decision that he made:

I don't discredit the medium in its ability to be pictorially interesting or appealing, but I think that it's a very low dynamic in the spectrum of television's qualities. I think the focus of the picture is always what people are interested in, and pretty pictures, per se, mean very little in terms of television's environment.

I may be wrong, you know. For example, I did *Rosenkavalier,* and the biggest single moment in the opera is the presentation of the rose. You have this enormous silver-white mylar set, with about five hundred people on stage, all dressed in brocade, and there's an enormous amount of fanfare, with people coming in, servants running around. Then you have Sophie about to accept the rose and Octavian coming in with the rose. The doors are thrown open, and musically it all works up to the biggest climax in the entire opera. You have about five chords—da, da, da, da, da—and on those five chords, that's the point everything is happening on stage.

At that moment, I decided to cut to a close-up of Octavian's hand holding the rose. Now that's a liberty that I am taking for television . . . someone

*Jean-Pierre Ponelle, one of the most successful of present-day operatic designers and directors, died on August 11, 1988, at the age of fifty-six.

sitting in the opera house is not going to be able to single out the hand with the rose at that moment.

It's obviously stretching the point, but here you have something called *Rosenkavalier,* and you've been singing about this damn rose for two acts, and here, the guy comes in and presents it. I just thought—well, this is what the opera is all about. This is the key moment, so I ought to be on the rose.

Nobody complained, but I think everyone involved in the production was aware of what I was doing. You know, a TV director imposing his judgment on all this.

One of the lovely paradoxes of Kirk's work is the changing level of involvement with what assignments he takes: starting some shows from scratch; catching up with others late in the production when they are complete entities. Most of the things that he does can be described as classical in nature—plays, operas, concerts—but I don't think that Kirk would be bored by anything. It might be interesting to follow him through a more populist piece, a sitcom or a rock concert. I am certain that he would not be bored. The variety of things that he concerns himself with when he is doing a show keeps him constantly connected with each and every program that he does. We talked about his early days as the director of the NBC Opera, when little was documented by way of "how to," yet Kirk prevailed.

At that time, the whole shebang was up to me. For better or worse, it all really started with the director. God, I even used to design all the sets. When I started to do opera, I really knew very little about it, so I really started with it as I would with a play—with the play's script, the libretto. And since I hadn't been preconditioned to a whole lot of opera performances, I had to build from there.

Fortunately, I was able to choose material that I was basically in tune with. I didn't try impossible operas. I selected things like *La Boheme.* You know, Puccini is especially gratifying for a director who's starting out because he's so theatrical. He leads you so comfortably into what's right. If I had started with *Parsifal,* I wouldn't have had any idea what to have done. Wagner would have been too much for me.

Anyway, I would try and get involved in the overall shape of the thing, where people are, what they have to do, the areas in which they function. You have so many opportunities in television that you don't have under the proscenium; a director is missing the boat if he thinks literally in stage terms. Of course, a lot of what we did depended on the amount of money that we had been given, which wasn't much in those days.

We continued our discussion, dwelling on the participation of the other people involved in the production of an opera: the conductor, the stage director, the chorus director, the choreographer:

The conductor starts right from scratch like I do, and if there is any conflict, it's usually resolved very early in rehearsal. Obviously, a conductor works within a certain framework that he is in complete control of, but when there's some flexibility in the musical line, some use of recitative, or where you have long firmatas,* what goes on on-stage can be different from what your picture is. How long is that firmata? Do you want five close-ups before the next thing happens? On stage, the action goes on because there is nothing else to do, but on camera, you have justification for some extra detail. Now, basically, the conductor controls all that, and the stage director has some input, but you are controlling what the audience at home is seeing.

In spite of all this, I don't think my vision ever comes through—nor should it necessarily. When you're doing it, you think it does, but when you look back on it, it's always less than you think.

We were coming to the end of our interview, and there were still several things that I wanted to cover—for one, how a director prepares for his shoots. Most directors do their "homework," more or less, but I had a hunch that no one did it more intensively than Kirk. A director who is at ease in the control room, going about his work with dispatch—well, you can always be assured that he is one who has prepared the best.

I have to be very well prepared. There are some directors that come in and just build a show as they are going along. I just am not secure unless I am totally prepared. I've learned over the years to be open to change. In other words, I come into the studio with an idea of what I want to do every single minute of the time I am there, but I am also prepared to throw it out if it doesn't work. I would be terrified if I didn't have a marked script, a finished show, when I got into the studio—every camera, every shot. My overall plan is to have something there when I first start rehearsal; then you can play around—some sequence, some camera trick you want to try—see how those things might work.

After a day's rehearsal, I go home at night, and on the strength of what I've seen that day—knowing what the performers are doing, what has worked and what hasn't—I re-mark my script.

---

*Firmata is a musical term for a rest or a hold, indicated by a symbol over the note to be held, usually subject to the interpretation of the artist or the conductor.

Finally, I wanted to quiz Kirk to find out how he felt about the "new wave" in television, the trend initiated by the look of rock concerts. The rock promoters wanted to send the same kind of psychedelic message that the attendant hordes received to a television audience, and the results are still with us. Not all of it is bad—some of the dynamic shooting, quick cutting, kooky lighting, and hand-held camera work does succeed to a degree. I just wanted to find out if Kirk was aware of any of this, and if it had any influence on his work.

I don't demean it, but I do think that a lot of it is "flash." It's very inventive, but ultimately, when you tell an audience that all things are possible, and they realize that all things are possible in terms of style—it's going to be very hard to keep interest going.

You do anything, just to be kooky. Turn pictures upside down, color faces purple, rotate them—anything. After you do that for 30 seconds, unless you're a great artist, unless you impose some discipline, what you have is just another visual gimmick.

I assumed that he would feel the same way about digital effects.

I look at these commercials where a flat plane becomes a three-dimensional surface, turning into a motor car and then into a refrigerator or a trip into outer space, and I haven't the vaguest idea of how it's all done.

But I don't think the audience really cares after a while, once they know it's all possible. We all know that machines can do anything, so what's so great? I want to know what you are supposed to feel about something—if something doesn't have any emotional or thought quality, it's lost. That's where the strength of the medium lies, not in its gimmickry.

I also asked him how he felt about the new technology. We are in an industry where every year the tools of our trade—the "state of the art"—change.

If they talk about it, I don't know what they're talking about most of the time. I went up to the studio for a survey on *Alice in Wonderland*,* and I was told that "We've installed a D–3–35 in here and you have 547 X's over there," and I haven't the remotest idea of what they are talking about. I say, "Well, as long as I can do my show and get pictures, I'm

*At the time of this interview, Kirk Browning was restaging *Alice* for public television. It was broadcast as part of the *Great Performances* series in the spring of 1984.

happy." But I don't know what the hell they are talking about most of the time. They say, "What kind of camera do you want, a TK76 or a TK83?" and I say, "Look, I want a camera that sends out great pictures. I don't give a damn what the number is."

I'm really terribly grounded in the old values of the close-up, the face, the feeling. I know that I'm probably missing the boat in some areas, but I just don't see any of these [technical] advances doing more than superficially glossing up the material.

My final question was, Where do you think television, as you have known it, is going—not only in the coverage of the arts, but in the medium as a whole?

Here I think technology will be important, but whatever happens, let's hope that it will be something that will make you appreciate what's inside the screen. Right now, I don't have any great hope that people's perceptions will grow with the medium. I think you can do good programs and you can do bad programs, but I don't think you're going to make a great dent in the public perception of television until the audience gets something brand new in the way of how the picture is received in the home. . . . I just wish they'd do something so that audiences had a little better opportunity to respond to the content in a show. It's awfully difficult to care about what's on television today, with the low definition on that small set in our living rooms.

Luckily, for everyone, Kirk Browning goes on doing the job he is so well suited for. The last time that we talked, he was on his way to Austria to do a documentary about the life of Wolfgang Amadeus Mozart for PBS. It should be broadcast in early 1990.

Prior to that, since our interview, his eclectic schedule in the arts has been filled with many wonderful projects, including a *Live from Lincoln Center* concert featuring the renowned flutist James Galway with the New York Philharmonic Orchestra. He is always off somewhere, endlessly energetic. He flew to Europe to direct soprano Leontyne Price in a production of Verdi's *La Forza del Destino* and to Australia to supervise the taping of *The Tales of Hoffman* with Dame Joan Sutherland at the Sydney Opera House—all in addition to his usual busy schedule at the Met, including a recent version of the controversial production of Puccini's *Turandot,* directed for the stage by Franco Zeffirelli. We wish Kirk continued success.

2

Sandy Grossman: Directing the Super Bowl

Directors of sports programs seem to have greater tenure than college professors. Sandy Grossman has been directing football and basketball at CBS Sports almost as long as the network has been producing these contests. Incidentally, it's hard to recall that there was a day when the CBS network had not recognized the profitability of sports as Sunday afternoon programming and gave that time over to public affairs programs like *Omnibus*.

Now Sandy Grossman and others like him stay committed to football and basketball, from the middle of August until the middle of May. Then, to saturate the networks (and now cable) even further, a whole other group of producers, directors and technicians begins in February to cover baseball for television, winding that down around the last week in October. Sports is big business on television and a year-round commitment.

Sandy Grossman graduated from the University of Alabama late in the fifties, his heart set on being a radio announcer. But after his discharge from the service, he migrated to New York and found work at WCBS–TV, the network's owned and affiliated station in the city, not as an announcer, but as a production assistant in television.

A couple of years as a PA at the local station proved Grossman's worth to his superiors, and in the midsixties, he moved over to the network and CBS Sports. It took five years for him to work his way

Portions of this chapter previously appeared in *Television Quarterly,* a publication of the Academy of Television Arts and Sciences, vol. 21, no. 3, 1985.

Sandy Grossman

up through the ranks to become an associate director. He remembers his first directing job very well:

> ... the guys at Sports wanted to see if I could direct, so they gave me the second period of a hockey game to do. At the end of the first period, the director just got up, and I sat down and called the shots for the second period. Unfortunately, when I got back to New York, nobody had seen the game. But I guess I hadn't screwed up too badly because I started doing the pre-game show on a regular basis, and then, the following year, I got a chance to direct some football.

It all seemed a little casual in the retelling as I sat with Grossman in the conference room at CBS Sports, high atop "Black Rock," the modernistic tower that houses the Columbia Broadcasting System on the Avenue of the Americas in New York City. After all, this was CBS's top director of sports programs, and outside of the setting, there was little glitz, no glamour and almost no ego to the man I was talking to.

He certainly doesn't look like he does what he does. He's short, rather unassuming and very up-front—more like a small-town lawyer than a sophisticated, "big-time" director of National Basketball Association tournaments and Super Bowls. I quickly got the impression that he was also someone who was not easily fazed outside of the control room. His is such a high-pressure, high-energy job, doing sports "live" on the CBS network, that I would assume he harnesses his kinetic power for those crucial moments in the booth or the remote truck when he is calling the shots on a game.

Because I did not know him personally, Grossman became a hard man for me to reach. I persisted through the press representative for CBS Sports, who was sympathetic to my project and arranged an interview. It took almost another month before Grossman's busy schedule had an open date, but all of this was quickly forgotten as I finally started to query him about his work.

My persistence in wanting to interview Sandy Grossman, rather than any one of the dozens of others at the networks or cable who direct sports, was, in fact, due to my own love of the game—I'm a rabid football fan—and my vivid recall of one shot I'd seen on a game called by Grossman. I don't remember who was playing whom. It doesn't really matter. But I do recall a shot of a huge, black defensive lineman, kneeling on the sidelines, holding his helmet, his face anguished with fatigue, covered with perspiration, waiting his turn while his team was on the offense.

The cameraman, obviously hand-holding his camera on the side-lines, framed this Herculean figure in the foreground, and the team's contest in the background. It was a magnificent shot, and the director held it for a long five seconds, choosing it instead of play action. That one shot embodied everything about the game that was meaningful to me: the magnificent contest, the clash of personalities, the tension. It was a majestic shot, and the director, unknown to me at the time, had chosen it instead of play action. It was ancient Rome and the glory of the gladiator all over again.

When the game finished, I watched the credits and for the first time became familiar with the name of Sandy Grossman, and when I started to do these interviews, I knew that I wanted to talk to him and no other when I discussed the aesthetics of covering sports.

I began by asking him who was in the normal cast of characters that covers a football game. He explained that the CBS network covered several professional games on a weekend, and that he was usually assigned to ex-player Pat Summerall and ex-coach John Madden:

One does play-by-play, the other is an analyst. Play-by-play, in the case of Summerall and Madden, is Pat Summerall . . . he does it from the snap of the ball to the moment it's down. He's the reporter; he describes what's happening on the field. John Madden is the analyst and color man; he brings in all the other aspects of the game: why a play worked, why it didn't, all the color. But it's the blend of these two, since Pat is also an analyst, that brings a lot of information to the telecast, and makes their coverage so good.

Pat is on his own; he knows what has to be done. What I will do is leave him sometimes on a shot I take. I will hit the key and say, "Hey, a shot of Youngblood" . . . "A shot of Landry"* . . . or whatever I'm going to take, just so he'll know this shot is coming up. Usually, that triggers some kind of response, something he's got in his head he might want to talk about.

But we were getting ahead of ourselves. I wanted him to give me a breakdown of just exactly what it took to do an NFL game, of how much preparation was involved. He does a game every week from the middle of August until March, if his network has the contract to cover the Super Bowl. I wanted to discover his normal routine for a game that wasn't the Super Bowl.

*Tom Landry was the coach of the Dallas Cowboys, and Jack Youngblood was one of his players.

Let's say that it's ten days before the game. I will already have checked with my people here in New York and gone over who my crew will be. On Monday morning of game week, I'll talk to the producer and review what we're going to be doing. Next I go to work on the details. That's mostly a lot of phone work; I find out who's going to play and who's not in shape, the condition of the field, and so on. By Thursday it's time to finalize whatever details remain incomplete.

On Friday, we go out to the remote site—normally our trucks arrive the same day, and they will have already started their initial setup: powering up, putting the cameras in position. We also meet with the [public relations] people.

On Saturday, we'd probably go to the home team practice, which is about eleven o'clock in the morning. The visiting team doesn't get in until maybe four or five o'clock in the afternoon and rarely practices on the site. We will talk to the coach first, maybe get an assistant coach to brief us. At the end of the practice, we'll go into a film session.

Summerall and Madden and myself, plus the producer, will screen game films of both teams from the preceding Sunday to see what they did the week before. Madden will point out things he notices that might translate into "isolation" shots for the next day. Anyway, we look at film for a couple of hours. Then we go back to the hotel and set up a meeting with the other team's coach. Somehow, we also manage to squeeze in a production meeting. Finally, we all go to dinner together and over the meal wrap up everything we're planning to do.

On Sunday, if it's a one o'clock game, I'm on the remote site by nine A.M. At that point, I'll probably have a camera meeting, spend about an hour with the cameramen, go over what each camera will be covering and what my isolation cameras are going to be doing. Next, I go up in the booth, check the pictures and make sure there are no problems. I take special care to make sure communications with all the technicians and the production people check out. Then we break for lunch. The talent will be there, and we fill them in. Next, we go over all the graphics—show everyone what we've prepared. Finally, we talk through the on-camera opening, get ready with the top of the show—maybe even record it.

I must say that I was surprised by the degree of Grossman's involvement. Nothing seemed to escape his concern, absolutely nothing. Television has always been described as a detail business. Almost every detail that you deal with has top priority. Just try misspelling one name on a list of show credits, and you will discover that truth for yourself. I was hearing an added something in what Grossman was telling me.

What happens is that certain actions on the field trigger certain other responses. I will give my cameramen and my videotape operators a sheet that says what we're going to do in certain routine situations; also what we do in goal line situations, punting situations, kickoffs, and goal line stands.

That process triggers off responses in everybody, and it's up to me to make sure that they are all doing what they are supposed to be doing.

I persisted, striving for more insights into what I perceived as his singularity. Was he the only man in communication with the cameras on the field? The answer was "Yes." Did he do all of his own "spotting"? Once again, the answer was "Yes." Then I asked about his A.D., his assistant director, what his function was there in the booth. I wondered if he was responsible for airing the instant replays. Grossman's response was most candid:

The assistant director has nothing to do with any of that. I make almost all of those decisions myself. The A.D. does most of his communicating with the stage managers and with the studio for commercials. It gets too confusing with another voice [in the booth] besides mine. Mine has to be the only voice when it comes to talking to the cameramen and the talent.

I finally began to get a picture of the controlled chaos that must be present in the booth at the top of the stadium or in the dark confines of the remote truck parked out back. I persevered, anxious to know more about the process:

Let's say it's a normal six-camera game. I rarely use more than that unless it's a play-off or a bowl game. You have a camera on the left 20-yard line, the 50-yard line, the right 20. High in the end zone will be a fourth camera; a golf cart on the sideline will hold the fifth, and number six will be hand-held, which can work anywhere. My instructions would call for any one of the cameras along the sideline, depending on where the teams are on the field, doing the play-by-play, Camera One shoots the far side receiver, and Camera Three takes the near side receiver or the defense. It changes with every situation on the field. What I essentially have is a three-camera show working the game, and whenever I call on Camera One, the others fall into place.

Of course, I will also do a lot of "winging" within that structure. I tell the crew before the game, this is just where I'm starting from. We'll jump off from there depending on what other things happen on the field. I also like to throw shots in that are just nice to look at.

I asked how much he counts on his cameramen to get shots for him.

I tell my three basic cameramen that from whistle to whistle, from the time play starts until it stops, they must do exactly what I tell them. Once the whistle is blown to start play, I want them to stay on those basic huddles. The other cameramen can hunt if they wish. If they hear the announcers talking about something over the phones, they go get that shot. . . . There are a lot of things that you'd like to shoot, but it often depends on just how creative your cameramen are. You can talk them through just so many shots; you can't talk them through good taste.

It all sounded terribly complicated to me. What a great drain this must be on someone like Grossman. I asked him if it helped when he was familiar with the crew he was working with.

Unfortunately, you don't always have the same cameramen every week. I've had cameramen who, when I said, "Get me the defensive huddle," would wind up on the *offensive* huddle. I've had people on camera that just didn't know the game, and I've had to talk them through every shot. You have the good and the bad, but you still have to make your game look right just the same—no matter who you've got out there.

Things change a bit when it comes to the play-offs. I handle my own crew, and I combine people I know from the East Coast and the West. I do the same for the Super Bowl. You just can't use people you don't know when you get into a situation where you are operating with twenty-four cameras and maybe twelve "isofeeds" for replays. The guys have to understand your system; you just can't break them in at the last minute.

Twenty-four cameras! My jaw fell. In all my years of working in television, and my involvement with hundreds of shows, I had never used more than five, and I had to think of the time I used that many.

All the cameras and VTRs have different functions. Maybe Camera Three in a normal game would have four or five—in the Super Bowl he'll have less. Each camera can be so much more exact, more specific on what it is going to get. With the Super Bowl, the same play you could only shoot *one* way before, when you had a normal complement of cameras, can now be shown in several different kinds of isolations and angles.

I commented on the intense amount of preparation that this must all take and wondered if he had ever gone into a situation where he had *no* preparation, where he had to "wing it."

Sure. But hopefully nobody else would know it. There are certain similarities with all football teams, and you get to know what those similarities
are, the strengths and weaknesses of the players, certain tendencies of the
teams and their coaches. For example, you keep in mind a certain key
defensive player that you know is going to react in a certain way, and
you're going to get some good replays on him. And you go with it.

Your game plan changes with each game, and with each set of announcers. You try to work off their strengths. When I work with Summerall
and Madden, I do the kind of replays that John Madden likes . . . he loves
the ones where the guys are groveling in the pits. It's the same kind of
excitement that he brings to the game. "My God, look at those guys!
They're biting, they're kicking, they're punching! I love it." That's his kind
of thing. He can also talk very intelligently about the finer aspects of the
game, but he excites the viewers when he get carried away by some of
those replays—especially when the guys are really bashing each other out
there. The one replay he never wants to see is a receiver going down ten
yards with nobody within a mile of him and all he does is turn around and
catch the ball. John told me once, "I won't even talk over that. Next time
I see that kind of boring replay, all you'll hear from me is heavy breathing."

I wanted badly to get into his involvement with aesthetics, so I
told Grossman why I had insisted on talking to him rather than any
other sports director. I repeated my perceptions of the lineman on
the sidelines and asked him if there were any aesthetic principles
that he applied to his work, or whether it was just a matter of
"eyeballing" something and then going with his reactive instincts.

You know, sometimes you'll take a shot on the kickoff, through the legs
of an official to the team kicking off, and it's a chancy shot; it might be
interesting to look, or it might be worthless. Worst of all, nobody in the
stands is watching from that point of view. But if I think it's pleasing, I
go with it. It's not something I want to do every time there's a kickoff,
but once in a while, I will throw in something like that. You know, storm
clouds coming up over the stands could be important—a weather problem
that could affect the game—but also very pretty to look at, like a sunset
in an evening game in San Diego, or a full moon, also beautiful to look
at. I think it adds something.

Grossman was obviously sensitive to a lot more that was going
on around him in the stadium than the game itself. Alert to everything, it appeared to me that he had two game plans going each
time he worked: the first was a highly technical one that involved
the actual coverage of the game; the second was the one that we

were discussing now, based on the emotional charge that he himself got out of the game, which he wanted to share with the audience.

I got knocked by one TV critic for Super Bowl XIV, which I am proud to say I won an Emmy* for. He said that some of my shots looked more like they belonged in a football movie than a football telecast. My only reaction was, What's wrong with that?

A creative cameraman can feed you a shot once in a while. Not all directors are looking for that kind of shot, but I encourage the guys I work with to look for them.

The Super Bowl that we did in Detroit in '83, even the player introductions were exciting as hell. I got great close-ups: you could see the guys' faces, their eyes; you could feel the drama in it. I had placed a mike right on the camera, and you could hear the players talking to each other on the field—it was terrific!

I even got permission from one of the teams to have an unmanned camera in the locker room, so that when John Madden said, in the pre-game show, that he was there with the players as they held their helmets waiting for the game to start and just couldn't wait to bust out, you got some idea of just how unbearable the pre-game tension was, and I knew that those were the kind of things that you've got to take a chance with if you want to convey the total impact of the game. And you can't get it just by pointing cameras at the game—you've got to feel what the emotions of the moment are.

It seems to me that most aesthetic reactions are drawn from your own personal and intellectual makeup—which is fine, except that in a television contest like a football game, which is interrupted constantly by commercials anyway, too much glitz and glitter might become distracting. I told Sandy that as a viewer, especially in a contest which I am following closely, I am distressed by too many shots of "crazies" in the stands, too many cutaways of the band, too many insertions of the Dallas Cowgirls. I wanted to know where he drew the line on this kind of color.

. . . in football, there are at least twenty seconds in between every play, and there are lots of things that you can show: the coaches, the huddles, the players; there's room for a great variety of things besides the game, and everyone has a different reaction to what you cut away to. There are some fans who don't want to see the audience; there are others who love it. It takes a little bit of everything to make a whole telecast.

*The statuette awarded by the National Academy of Television Arts and Sciences for excellence in television.

I think pretty girls are a very important part of that total picture. We get lots of letters from fans telling us how much they love the Dallas Cowgirls—it's important to them; it makes their Sunday afternoon more enjoyable. Then, on the other hand, we get lots of hate mail from people who say that they can't stand them.

. . . one of the most exciting shots in the '83 Detroit Super Bowl was of a woman in the stands who must have been at least eighty years old. She was wearing a San Francisco '49er sweatshirt and holding up one of those souvenir fingers, saying "We're #1." You could tell—something about her—she was a real fan, not a crazy.

Or take the NBA Championship last year, when I had pandemonium on the basketball floor—people standing up, screaming, yelling, carrying on. I dissolved to a little kid who was sleeping. It kind of put everything into perspective. Things like that are going on all the time at sporting events, and if you're sitting at home, I think you want to see them.

I do talk to the cameras about the kind of crowd they can get, and they are very good about picking their shots. The camera has a fatal fascination for people, and there are some who are always trying to "mug" the camera. You'll see them in every arena or stadium. You'll see the guys with multicolored hair, or the kids with the painted faces, the guys with the obscene T-shirts—the "kooks." There's one woman who sends me pictures and letters and shows up at every game; she could be a sporting event all by herself. She calls herself "Miss Body Beautiful," and, of course, I avoid her like the plague.

About the time that I interviewed Sandy Grossman, I had occasion to be present at my first New York Giant game in many years. At one time, many years ago, before the advent of intensive TV coverge, I had season passes, but when the Giants went into one of their periodic declines, I had given them up. Now I was watching the game in the stadium with new eyes, and I must admit there were some surprises. Long moments in the stadium, just sitting there, watching the teams standing around, doing nothing. In spite of the fact that I had worked in television most of my adult life, it took me several moments to figure it out. These were the times when one of the referees, acting as stage manager, had stopped play on the field so that the commercials could be cued for the home viewer. I must admit that I was shocked at the brazen intrusiveness of the act of stopping the game's progress. I asked Sandy if there were any other changes in the game as a result of television.

I've had the same reaction. I've sat in the stands myself, and I've said, "Damn those television guys!" But TV hasn't changed the game that much.

The networks might have put in a few more commercials over the years, but look, there is a profit motive. If the NFL were to say, "We'll cut the price of those rights in half, if you will cut back on the number of commercials," we could do it. But they're not going to do it, so we can't do it. It's the price the viewer pays for watching the game at home, free.

The fact is that there are many more subtle changes that have come about in sports as a direct result of television beyond simply interrupting play in a game. The "grandstanding," for example, playing to the crowd: the "high fives," the little dances in the end zone after touchdowns and long passes, emotions that run higher or lower than normal when a camera is present. Ten years ago you never saw a player spike a football in the end zone; now you are surprised when they don't. Grossman agreed with me—to some extent.

The kinds of kids that are playing now are different—they grew up with television. They're all show business, a different breed. In the old days, you had athletes that couldn't even talk; many of them were good old farm boys. Now they're more outgoing, and most of them get through college. They're all talking, and they're all doing better. They expect to be on camera in post-game interviews. Some of them even expect to have careers in television or in public affairs when their playing careers are over.

And it's not just their public appearances, for the caliber of the athletes has improved every year. They're running faster and jumping higher. Linemen are running as fast as the backs used to run twenty years ago.

Where is all of this going? Will television sports coverage change in the future?

There's no way I can answer that, just like no one could foresee twenty years ago what the instant replay would do to television sports. The new technology will play an important part. Look at the lenses we are using now. With almost no light, we can get tighter close-ups and better close-ups with each succeeding year. The equipment is getting smaller, and the lenses are getting more powerful, and the result is that we are going places and seeing things that we could never reach before or see before. And there are still tremendous technical advances going on.

I left "Black Rock" filled with admiration for Sandy Grossman. You knew that whatever technical change time would bring, men like Grossman would find the ways to utilize that change with intelligence.

The last thing I asked him dealt with his own future: Did he want to continue in sports, or were there other things in television that he would like to try? He told me that he felt that there were other things "geared" for a sports director, and he thought that he would like to do some of those things, like the Miss America Pageant, the Oscars, the Emmys. But I still see Grossman's credit whenever I watch a football or basketball game on the CBS network. Someone is missing a bet in not moving him out of the stadium, but I guess that he's too valuable a franchise where he sits, and I'm sure that everyone at CBS knows it.

3

George Schaefer: Directing
Hallmark Hall of Fame

George Schaefer is an amazing success story. I don't think he's ever put his hand to a project that doesn't establish his taste both as a producer and as a director. Now, that can be said about almost everyone in our business to a degree, but George is more, much more—he is a tastemaker, someone who has defined the boundaries of television. And in a business which has often been described as one which settles for the lowest common denominator in public taste, that is really unique—setting cultural goals for oneself, and more often than not fulfilling them. Like everyone in show business, George has had his successes and his failures, but I can't think of anyone in television whose artistic perceptions have been so consistently on the line in his forty years of working in the medium, much of that time producing and directing the *Hallmark Hall of Fame,* the longest-running dramatic series in television.

We sat in his office in the San Fernando Valley, where among his neighbors are some of the huge studios that service the motion picture and television industry, and talked about those forty years of creativity. He seemed particularly engaging on the day we talked, turned on by his retrospection, I assumed, because he was moving crosstown, about to assume the prestigious chairmanship of the Theatre, Film, and Television Department at UCLA, and he must have been counting his blessings.

How did it all begin? Most of his early professional life had been spent in New York City, on Broadway, directing, producing and

Portions of this chapter previously appeared in *Television Quarterly,* a publication of the Academy of Television Arts and Sciences, vol. 23, no. 2, 1988.

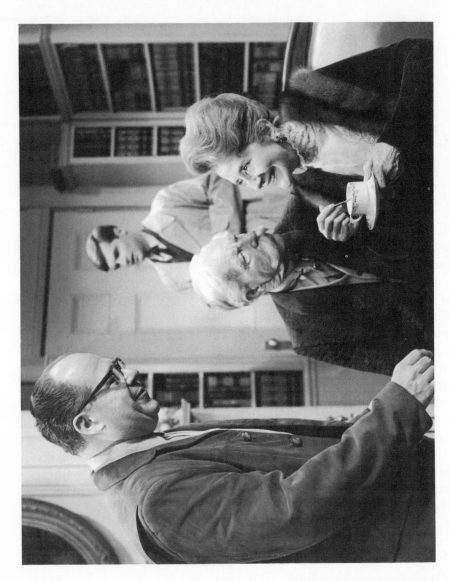

George Schaefer (left) directing Alfred Lunt and Lynn Fontanne in *The Magnificent Yankee*.

occasionally lighting shows. But then he told me he had started watching some of the early television programs and was fascinated with the medium's possibilities.

Mildred Freed Alberg, who worked in the promotion department at one of the networks and was a very bright young woman, asked Maurice Evans if he would be interested in doing a production of *Hamlet*, which I had directed for him on Broadway and was known as the *G.I. Hamlet*, as a television show.

Evans was intrigued with the idea, as I was, so the three of us spent part of that summer (Maurice was actually touring in a production of Shaw's *Devil's Disciple* that I had co-produced with him at the City Center) looking for ways to do the *G.I. Hamlet* on television.

It was Millie who made the breakthrough. She contacted Foote, Cone, and Belding, the agency for Hallmark Cards, and eventually got through to Mr. J. C. Hall himself.

The result was a two-hour live TV production of *Hamlet,* my first encounter with television. I didn't shoot the show; I only directed the actors; the technical part of television and the control room still intimidated me. Albert McCleery called the shots. He had been producing and directing a series of half-hour weekly dramas for Hallmark, and he knew the medium backwards and forwards, so we split the directional job—I staged it, he shot it.

And it was a huge success. Goodness knows it had its failings, but it reached a huge audience, made Hallmark want to continue doing plays for television. So we went ahead, Millie, Maurice, and I, and did two more Shakespearean plays: *Richard II* in the following year and a production of *Macbeth* in the third year.

By the time of that third program, *Macbeth,* George was directing the whole shebang, cameras and actors alike, enjoying every minute of it, and Hallmark, buoyed by the success of its first three programs with Evans, Alberg, and Schaefer, decided to make a full-time commitment to television with them. Evans and Alberg were to produce; Schaefer was to direct. He continued the story:

Strangely, Maurice was not that happy about it. He felt that he was personally responsible as producer, but he also felt he had very little control. So he withdrew from the series after the first year.

Hallmark wanted more, so Mildred Alberg and I formed a company called Milberg Productions to continue producing the *Hallmark Hall of Fame,* and as you know, the program thrived for a number of very successful years.

Then Millie and I went in different directions. She wanted to get more involved in the artistic end of things, which I felt was really my province. So I said fine, and I signed a contract to go to Hollywood and make movies for MGM.

Well, to put it mildly, Hallmark was very upset. They sent emissaries to me and said, "Look, you can't do this to us. Everything is going gloriously. It's the best show on television; we're excited about it. What's the problem? What will convince you to stay?"

So I said, "Well, I guess if I could form my own company, with a handful of the people that I want to work with, and produce the *Hallmark Hall of Fame* exclusively—I would enjoy that. Let me see if MGM will let me out of my contract."

Well, William Morris, my agent, had hysterics at the time, but went back and talked to the heads of MGM, who were very understanding. And they told him, "Look, if Schaefer ends up working for another film company, we'll sue you. But if he just continues to do *Hallmarks* on television, we'll release him from the contract."

And they did. I formed Compass Productions, and we moved into some of the great years with Hallmark, which continued until I'd done over sixty shows for them.

Those Hallmark years were the happiest, the most productive, the most successful ones of my life. A way of working that no longer exists. When I tell friends working in television today how I functioned, they shake their heads and don't believe it.

I'd fly down to Kansas City for a two-day meeting at the beginning of the summer, discuss the various properties that the agency and my Compass gang had worked on together and suggest our schedule for the year. J. C. would ask a few questions, think about our choices, and a couple of days later he'd call up and say, "Those are the five or six shows I think we should do this year." And that was it.

We worked in an atmosphere of complete artistic freedom. The network had nothing whatsoever to say about what we did. We would have one meeting with them regarding how they would promote and publicize the programs, and that was it.

Television is a very deceptive medium, especially for the home viewers who watch so much of it. It almost becomes a part of their persona, and subconsciously they feel a synthesis with the screen that is unique—it doesn't happen when they attend a movie or go to the theatre. It makes the process of creating shows on TV appear easy, especially now with home video cameras falling into more and more consumer hands. Well, the fact is that it isn't. Doing a program, getting it right, it is considerable chore that requires great skill. I asked George about his transition, about the first time that he moved from the stage into the control room. I was interested in whether it was difficult for him to learn enough so that he could function:

> ... the first thing that you've got to do when you think about any kind of live TV or taped drama is forget the total picture, and remember that you're dealing in small segments—in close-ups. You're dealing in heads and bodies, hands and objects, ... twosomes, and threesomes, over-the-shoulder shots, fragments and reactions, rather than the breadth and width of the proscenium that you deal with in a theatre.
>
> So what you do is to break down what in the theatre would be a single unified experience into two, three, four hundred small pieces, which, when they go together, are hopefully as powerful, maybe even more powerful than a stage performance would be.
>
> This can be a big hazard for a new director. It was not for me—I think, primarily, because of my bridge playing. I love tournament bridge, and when you're playing bridge, every hand, fifty-two different elements are juggled around, juxtaposed, in ever-changing patterns.
>
> A bridge player's mind is adjusted to that kind of fragmentation, so that I really had no problem in handling multiple lenses and cameras. In fact, I miss the camera when I direct for the theatre.
>
> In theatre, I start small, usually meeting in the intimacy of a rehearsal room, searching for truth, for honesty and for motivations. But when I finally get the play on the stage (particularly the last two which I've done out here in L.A. in the huge Ahmanson Theatre), I'm forced to expand on whatever reality I've found. At that point I can't help thinking about what television can do—I'd love to have caught some idea with a tight close-up or made sure everybody in the audience was watching the exact detail that I was showing and not the whole stage.

Most young directors cut just for the joy of cutting, forgetting that every time you cut, you are making an editorial decision—and a very strong one. If you are videotaping a play, your decisions are crucial to the content and the development of that play. During rehearsals, and your subsequent blocking, a close study should be made of the author's intentions and the thrust of his play, a study that should lead to the conclusions that are made in relation to your blocking of that play.

Reaction shots are even more important: what you select and how close you are in your selection. I recently viewed the Democratic National Convention meeting in Atlanta (July 1988), and I watched the keynote address of Ann Richards, a skilled politician and speaker. I thought it was a rather lightweight effort, but in the television coverage, she came across magnificently, due primarily to the efforts of the director covering the convention—I think I was watching ABC's transmission. He was masterful in his use of "cut-away" shots, reaching into the auditorium for extraordinary reactions, accenting every point that Ms. Richards made, enlarging the speech into a major address. The camera is a powerful tool when used intelligently.

You can do an awful lot of things with a camera that you can't do on stage. For one thing, you can protect performers. Last year I did a Christmas film in Canada with all young children in it. And one little girl, a precious thing, had never acted before. One of her big scenes was to be with Loretta Swit, and it was conceived as a series of close-ups cutting back and forth between them. The little girl just couldn't do it, but Loretta held her concentration, and we got *her* performance on film. So I sent Loretta home, and I worked alone with the girl, feeding her cues. We did her lines over and over again, repeating each speech until we finally got those four or five or six words just right. When we put the scene together, it seemed effortless and was most effective.

I've always felt comfortable with cameras, even in the days of live television. That was wonderfully exciting, like flying a small airplane with a coughing motor, never sure you were going to be able to land safely.

There would be any number of hazards, whether it was studio noise, or somebody going up in their lines, or crossing where they shouldn't, or some technical foul-up.

You had to adjust when things went wrong, and very often would have to make quick, on-the-spot decisions: "Cancel shots 98 and 99. We're going directly to 100, but be wider. Get ready for 101 because you're gonna have to be further left and much tighter." And when you got back in the pattern, back to your shots list with much relief, before you knew it the show would be over. It was all very exciting.

At the end of those live shows, you were on a real high. I mean, it took a whole evening to settle down again.

Strangely, the major networks each use a different system by which their director communicates with cameramen in the studio and on location. NBC and ABC, at one time, prior to their enforced separation by the Federal Communications Commission, were both parts of the same company, operating under similar agreements with the union that their technicians belonged to: NABET, the National Association of Broadcast Engineers and Technicians. After a particularly rancorous strike many years ago, a very strict mode of functioning in the control room was mandated in which the director was allowed to communicate with his cameramen only through the technical director. This necessitated the development of a very strict, highly inflexible list of shots. I always thought that it stultified creativity and slowed the directorial process down to a halt. This policy met with strong opposition from the Director's Guild and was eventually changed.

Conversely, at CBS, operating through a different technical union, IBEW, the International Brotherhood of Electrical Workers, the situation was much more relaxed. Directors talked to the studio floor, directly to their cameramen, or through associate directors who prepared shots. (Directors at the three major networks, incidentally, are all members of the Director's Guild of America.)

As the business has become more fragmented—because of expansion by new companies, new broadcast coalitions and alliances, new modes of program distribution—directors are becoming more flexible, learning how to function under any and all systems. I asked George about the difference obvious to him as he went from NBC to CBS in his travels.

I grew up in the NBC system; I preferred it, although many directors did not. I would make out a numbered shot sheet for each camera after I had completed my blocking in the rehearsal hall. Once we were in the studio, the technical director would punch up whatever I would call for on my shot sheet.

In the CBS system you don't number your shots. I continued to do so because it was the only way I could do a show, but it didn't mean very much to them at CBS. The technical director there would be in charge of all the technical things, but would not talk to the cameramen the way they did at NBC.

The associate directors at CBS were the key men. They would keep up a running conversation with the cameramen, describing the shots coming up for them, but not using numbers. They would say: "Camera Three, coming to an over-the-shoulder shot. Camera Two, coming to wide shot; hold the shot when they break. Camera One, coming to close-up." I would still be calling the shots with a snap of my finger to the T.D. beside me, but the readying of them was being done by the A.D. I never felt it was quite as precise, but it was equally effective.

I must admit that it was a more flexible system. In times of disaster, you could swing with the CBS system, whereas at NBC, there was a certain amount of rigidity.

But . . . they both worked.

I continued to talk to George about the rehearsal process. His early start in the industry had given him a wide-ranging view of almost every potential function as a director. We talked a good deal about working in "live" television.

It's paradoxical today that many young directors break into the business working "live"—doing the news, sports, special events, at local stations. The directors who follow their hearts to Hollywood, where more than 90 percent of the network drama is produced, rarely see a situation where they are working "live." They've even created a peculiar description for some of their work: "live on tape." It sounds like an oxymoron to me.

George went on to describe what it was like to rehearse and present a show in the early days of television:

With live shows, you were always fighting time. We would rarely have more than four days in the studio. The first day and a half would be blocking. I would block in segments. By the afternoon of the second day, I could stagger through a complete performance—sort of stop and go— just getting the bugs out. On the third day, we'd have two dress rehearsals. The second dress rehearsal would usually be a pretty darned good approximation of the performance, as close as we could get before the air show.

After that third day I would go home, take a short nap, and then work, sometimes till three or four in the morning, going through the script, shot by shot, page by page, remembering. I'm very good at this for some reason. I could remember everything I'd seen on all the monitors that afternoon; I'd have complete recall.

I would make extensive notes, for the cast on one pad and for the technicians on another. Then on the morning of the air show—remember this was all to be aired live—I'd meet first with the cameramen and the technicians.

I, or an assistant of mine, had prepared new shot sheets for each camera, and because we were talking the same shorthand, we'd go very quickly.

Then I would meet with my actors, prior to our final dress rehearsal— a meeting which hopefully incorporated all my notes. Very rarely did I make any changes between the final dress rehearsal and air because there were too many interdependent elements; every time I would change one, another would be effected. And you don't want surprises when you are on the air live.

No "surprises." How delighted I was to hear Schaefer say it because, more than any other expression, it has been the catch phrase in my attempts in these last eight years to steer students through the vicissitudes of producing and directing television programs. I say it all the time as something I expect from them—"no surprises!"

There is something in the nature of the process that gives birth to arrogance in the uninitiated. The less one knows, the more likely he is to try something in the studio based on the seat of his pants and nothing else. Everything that happens in the studio will more than likely happen in the process of pre-production, when time is your ally; then, and only then, can you deal with problems easily. It's called rehearsal. When you are in the studio, time is your enemy, and if you are not prepared, the show suffers. No surprises!

George and I went on to discuss the two weeks of rehearsal it took him to do his *Hallmark Hall of Fame* productions. I commented that it seemed like a relatively short time to get a full play ready for television.

Well, it really isn't. There was more rehearsal time in those fourteen days than I've ever had on Broadway. The *Hallmarks* were ninety-minute shows, which meant seventy-five minutes of playing time. And for those seventy-five minutes we had a nineteen-day work schedule, with two days off.

Your average Broadway play runs two-and-a-half hours, minus any intermissions, which gives you two hours and ten minutes of running time, as against those seventy-five minutes on television.

On a Broadway play you will get four weeks of rehearsal. But still, the last week was almost entirely spent on getting out of town, breaking in the set, getting the technical stuff right. I always found that I had enough time on television.

In fact, when directing with a single camera, it's only on the night before I shoot that I plan my next day's schedule—somewhere between twenty and thirty setups.

Several years ago, I was pleased to discover that I was not alone in my method from reading an article in the *American Film Institute* magazine about Ingmar Bergman, describing his way of working. He said: "I wait until the night before, and then, with all the elements at my fingertips, I plan what I will shoot the next day."

In George Schaefer's long and rich career producing and directing plays for television and the theatre, he has always been very discriminating in his selection of talent, looking for the best and getting them. He has brought to television some of the outstanding theatrical and cinematic lights—stars such as the Lunts, Julie Harris, Mary

Martin, Bette Davis, Christopher Plummer and Katherine Hepburn, among many others, all of whom have enjoyed a close working relationship with him.

George told me of some of *his* experiences in dealing with talent, and I was impressed by his sensitivity in this important aspect of his work—he really didn't want to tell me whom he thought was the finest actor or actress he had ever worked with, and he fudged the question, wisely never really answering it:

I'm rarely disappointed by the big stars, very rarely, because they're all, you know, quite extraordinary people. Most talented.

He finally, reluctantly, told me two stories—the first was about Lynn Fontanne and Alfred Lunt, two of the great talents of the American theatre; the second was about Julie Harris. Both stories, I think, gave me more insight into George Schaefer than the stars he was telling me about.

The Lunts were in a world of their own. One of the last times I was in Wisconsin visiting with them, Alfred was already weakened by illness. It was after lunch, and Lynnie had gone up to do some sewing, and Alfred and I were just chatting.

And out of left field, he said, "You know, among the many things I regret not being able to do any more, there is . . . nothing that I regret more than that I'm not going to be able to have you direct me again"— which just knocked me out. I mean, you can nourish your whole career on something like that because he was the giant of them all, a truly inspired actor.

My personal favorite is Julie Harris. We've done sixteen productions together, both in the theatre and in television.

Julie is the perfect actress, but has one failing. She loves to cry and feels that the audience is not moved if she doesn't.

When she starred in *The Last of Mrs. Lincoln* on Broadway, she gave a staggering performance. But she felt her opening night performance was just terrible because she hadn't cried in a certain scene that she sometimes had cried in. The audience sobbed, but that wasn't enough for Julie.

When we taped the show on PBS, there's a long eight-minute speech which she did in just one take. And we shot it twice. The second time, I was thrilled, thought it could not be better. But Julie said, "Oh, it's not any good, George. I know I can do it better." So I said, "All right, darling, tomorrow morning, nice and fresh, come in, we'll do it all over again. Now let's go on to something else."

So the next morning we did it, and she cried voluminously, and she was very happy with it. I studied the two performances and, of course, used the one from the night before. And when she saw it on the air, she said she loved it. I don't know whether she really did. I don't even know whether she knew that it was the take that she had been so upset about the day before.

There has been much debate over the years as to the efficacy of using tape or film in the production of programs. At the local station level, in the past ten years, we have seen film disappear completely in the production of news and public affairs. At the network level, only *60 Minutes* remains, still producing on film, an archaic link to the past.

I have always felt that tape and film were each equally viable, the real culprits being time and money. Using tape, we see an image instantaneously and go with it, and that pleases the cost accountants, but in the process we usually light imperfectly, underrehearse, and shoot carelessly.

I was anxious to learn George's feelings about this controversy, for he was someone who had seen and experienced it all, from directing live in studios to working on major motion pictures. I asked him if he was equally at home in both film and videotape.

The material usually dictates which would be better.

The first full-length film I ever did was *Macbeth* which was done for Hallmark, which, incidentally, was also the first movie ever made for TV . . . in the early sixties. We got the idea of taking the money that would be spent on a live TV show and going to Europe to make a very low budget movie. Maurice Evans and Dame Judith Anderson starred in it with a fabulous English cast: Michael Hordern, Malcolm Kean, George Rose.

But the most exciting thing was that we had Freddie Young who, at the time, was probably the world's best cinematographer. We had an incredible production team, and since this was my first movie, I needed them all.

The film itself was very successful on television and has been widely distributed since, particularly in schools and colleges. It's the only *Macbeth* film that ever made money.

Then I asked him if he were to shoot the same piece on both film and videotape, what he would do differently in each. In other words, had he ever shot something on film and then been sorry, thinking that it should have been done on videotape?

It's very interesting that you asked that because I have my *Macbeth* that I did live in the studio and *Macbeth* that I filmed. And you can run them side by side and see what some of the differences were.

I always wanted the TV Academy to do a series of evenings in which they would do that—take works that had been done in various media and compare them.

For example, *Johnny Belinda* was made as a fantastic film with Jane Wyman and Lew Ayres. Jean Negulesco was the director—a really beautiful film. Then I did *Johnny Belinda* live on *Hallmark,* with Chris Plummer and Julie Harris. We had a wonderful supporting cast, including Rip Torn and Victor Jory. I thought it was an excellent example of live, electronic television.

And, finally, Paul Bogart did a very interesting production with Mia Farrow, on tape. All three of these shows still exist. They wouldn't have to screen the whole picture, but perhaps three excerpts from identical scenes, discuss the differences and see what was most effective.

Each way of working has its strengths and its weaknesses. Whenever you are in production, there are certain limitations that you, as a director, immediately sense, that you have to live with, do the best you can and hope it's good enough.

But I feel that tape should not be used as film. If you're gonna film, film, but if you're gonna tape, take advantage of the same values that you get in a live performance. When taping, I break my script down into as few scenes as possible, and try to follow much the same schedule as with a live show.

But, instead of dress rehearsing the whole performance, as we did when we worked live, I block, dress, and shoot each one of the scenes as a separate entity.

If a scene runs seven, eight minutes, we'll do a rehearsal, take notes, block cameras, and then run it. Usually I'll do three takes, three complete versions of the scene.

Then I take the best parts of those three scenes and build my show. And I rarely find in those three takes that I am not covered. Of course, I have somebody checking, and occasionally they'll say, "This speech in the middle of page twelve on all three takes, she's gotten it backwards or said the wrong name, or it doesn't work." Then I'll do a pickup of that speech and edit it in. But those pickups usually look like pickups, as you don't get the excitement that comes from a sustained performance.

If I'm gonna film, that's something else again. There, I expect to do it all with one camera, to spend all day getting two or three minutes on film. And there is a whole other kind of energy, excitement and a try for perfection that you don't get with tape. The perfection that film offers is very satisfying, although I still enjoy the performance values that I get with videotape.

In spite of his patience, I thought it was wiser to pick up the pace a bit, knowing that I had intruded enough. I felt that there was just time for about a half-dozen more questions. How did he feel about cutting? For example, was he addicted to lots of quick cuts and reaction shots, or was he fond of long developing shots?

Those decisions depend entirely on the material. I think it's wrong to superimpose a shooting style on material that doesn't warrant it. Generally speaking, I respect the scripts I direct. I'm not a director who picks up a script and says, "This is a piece of cheese, but I will try and make it work."

I admire directors like Brian de Palma, for example, or Nicholas Roeg. They can take something that I would turn down as material and make a terrific movie out of it by imposing their own visual style and cinema sense onto something that really isn't that good. I can't do that.

When videotaping, Schaefer indicated that he usually picked up a scene in no more than three takes. So I asked whether he was against doing a lot of takes, doing a scene over and over again, hoping for that perfect take. Does it ever exist—that perfect take?

On film it does, yes. You think nothing of doing fourteen or fifteen takes in film. For one thing, you've spent forty-five minutes getting everything right for that forty seconds that you're shooting, and you're gonna get that forty seconds right or know the reason why. It's easy enough to say, "Cut, do it again." It's silly to settle for anything less than perfection in film.

While I was waiting in Schaefer's office prior to our interview, I noticed a brochure advertising for distribution some of the old *Hallmark* shows. As I read it, I assumed that he had gone through the long and difficult process of clearing the rights for both the talent and the scripts. I wondered if there had been any technical problems in making these old shows into new ones, and I asked George about that.

It was an exciting experience going back to shows done fifteen, twenty years ago, and seeing things I hadn't liked, and finding I can now correct them. You can even get rid of boom shadows. There's a thing called the Quantel, with which you actually recompose your shots.

There's one scene in *Victoria Regina* where we shot off the set. Every time I would see Victoria, I'd say, "Oh God, that's awful." It's a beautiful scene, but we shot off the set. Well, suddenly, you put it through the Quantel, and you recompose it, and you're not shooting off the set anymore. One is able to correct 90 percent of the things that went wrong, technically, on all of those shows, by just spending the time and the money.

He had obviously found some of the new technical developments in television adaptable and usable.

Indeed, . . . on the film that we made for HBO last year—*Right of Way* with Bette Davis, Jimmy Stewart and Melinda Dillon . . . it was shot beautifully, I must say. The cinematographer . . . Howard Schwartz did a brilliant job on it. And we took as much time as we needed. It was the most carefully produced feature that I had ever worked on. Jimmy Stewart said he'd never seen a feature more carefully lighted.

Yet, when it went on the air, HBO had the lab transfer the film print to tape. I didn't like the first transfer, so we had a second negative made, an interpositive, and took it to a magic machine, and went through it shot by shot, and on every single frame the technician balanced the picture electronically, with the cinematographer sitting alongside him, and they ended up with a tape absolutely true to the original colors.

On that machine, they can change the color of clothing, or they can change the sky, or the skin tones—all separately. They push little buttons, and they can alter anything they want from cut to cut. All it takes is time and money. It's a new world to me; it's just amazing what they can do. This is completely different than the disgusting attempts to put pasty color on black-and-white movies.

Coming to a close, hearing about the rebirth of some *Hallmarks* in their new and technically advantaged incarnation, I was curious about its network demise under *his* aegis after its long and successful run. (By the way, for all the readers and viewers who might be confused, *Hallmark* is still on the air several times a year, coincidental with various greeting card seasons, but under different production auspices.)

My life with Hallmark came to an end for a number of reasons. For one thing we'd begun to run out of plays that everybody could agree upon. Hallmark was not strong on original drama, for example, which I was very eager to do. They passed on an awful lot of wonderful original plays that we developed for them.

Then, too, there was Mr. J. C. Hall, himself. He was the spark plug behind the whole program. A wonderful man—he made all the key decisions himself. He retired, and his son, who was running the company brilliantly, was less interested in theatrical decisions. A committee took over, and the agency began to get more involved. It all came to a head for me over *The Visit*.

Lynn Fontanne and Alfred Lunt, who had done *Magnificent Yankee* for us (Lynn had also done *Anastasia* for *Hallmark*) wanted very much to do

The Visit, the Friedrich Duerrenmatt play they played so magnificently on Broadway. It had been bought and done as a "so-so" movie by 20th Century Fox with Ingrid Bergman and Anthony Quinn, and the Lunts were not happy about the movie, wanted to repeat their stage performances for television. So I went to Bill Self, who was in charge at Fox at the time, and he cleared the rights for the Lunts to do a TV performance.

They were excited about it, and I flew to Kansas City and got Hallmark's okay.

So everything was riding high. Got back, and a week later, the agency called and said, "You know, we've thought about it, and we decided we really can't sell Mother's Day cards with *The Visit.* In any event, we're not going to do it."

I was furious. Mike Dann was running CBS at that time. And Mike had been wooing me for various projects. So I went to Mike, and said, "Look what I've got, the Lunts in *The Visit.*" He said, "Great, fantastic" . . . two days later, he called: "I talked to my board. We lost so much money on *Death of a Salesman* last year, they won't let me do another arty show."

So that fabulous performance was lost to the world. And I thought, this is pretty dumb. If I'm going to devote my whole life to working in television and for the Hallmark Company . . . and yet when something like this comes along, I haven't got enough clout to get it on . . . I'm barking up the wrong tree. So at that point, I backed off and we moved to Los Angeles.

His move to California was obviously a very successful one. He still continues to produce, direct, win awards for his work and play lots of bridge. Even though he is in his late sixties, he seems to have little or no plans for easing off, although he is financially independent. He described his future to me in the most promising of terms.

Merrill Karpf and I just started this new company last year, and the general idea was to shoot for a decade of pleasant things, things that hopefully I can do as well or better than others, things that excite and challenge me. We're developing a lot of them, but whether I'll get to do them or not, I don't know. The plan was that it would be more interesting to have more control of one's fate than just to sit around and wait for people to come to you and ask you to do things. I shouldn't complain; I've been offered, I guess, a majority of the shows I would have wanted to do.

I also want to keep a finger in theatre. I hope at least once every two years I can do a play, if not for Broadway, for someone out here. And, most of all, to continue to work with exciting people.

He has succeeded in most of his goals as far as I can see. His film *Mrs. Delafield Wants to Marry* starring Katherine Hepburn was a finalist in the 1988 Director's Guild awards. On a visit to Los Angeles last spring, I noticed on the entertainment pages that he had revived two musicals for the theatre. Finally, and most prestigiously, he was appointed by Ronald Reagan to serve a six-year term on the National Council of the Arts. What a nice career, and what a lovely man.

4

Marc Daniels: Directing
I Love Lucy

Marc Daniels is one of the more pragmatic men I've ever met in my life—he creates television programs the way that other men undergo their morning ablutions. He's a "no nonsense" kind of guy—what you see is what you get. There's nothing devious about Marc; I don't think that he has a neurotic bone in his body, and if he does, he saves it for more cloistered moments than those obvious ones when he is directing a television show.

But I don't mean to imply by this that his approach to his art is casual. As a producer, you know from the first time you place a script in his hands that your project is going to be handled with taste and without temperament. There is no arrogance in what Marc does, no brandishment of personality. He moves easily and quickly in the studio. Watching him work, I'm always impressed by his ease with actors and the respect that they have for him. Paradoxically, his approach is almost totally nonintellectual: this is the show; let's get on with it. Most of my academic colleagues who try to take the literature of the theatre and television into the studio would not quite know what to make of someone like Marc Daniels.

I've known him longer than any of the other men that I've interviewed for this collection. Our relationship has been almost purely professional, but I have spent many pleasant moments in Marc's company and consider him a friend. We first met in 1948 when I was working as a director for NBC radio, beginning to feel the need to discover something about that thing called television that was slowly displacing me at 30 Rockefeller Plaza in New York City. I read somewhere that the American Theatre Wing, which had done

Marc Daniels on the set with Cathleen Nesbitt and Maureen O'Hara.

such splendid work during World War II entertaining G.I.s through such institutions as the Stage Door Canteen, was now directing its efforts into training some of those ex-soldiers and ex-sailors for work in the theatre—and the new medium of television. I decided to take one of those courses—the cost was nil, the teacher was Marc Daniels. I asked him about this and his early entree into television.

The year was 1947, and like yourself, I decided to take a course in television production given by the American Theatre Wing, which was taught at a small experimental station in Jamaica, Long Island. It wasn't much; the station had three cameras, a control panel, an audio board, not much more—all built by the man who owned the station.

The class was taught by someone named Harvey Marlowe. You may remember him; he was one of the first TV directors in New York—I think he worked for Dumont.

I was on the faculty of the Wing teaching *theatre* courses, but being a G.I., I was also entitled to *take* courses, so I took this course in television production. Harvey lectured to us, and sort of told us how to do it. Then he divided the class up into two groups and said each group would put on a small scene every other session. Then he pointed to me, since he knew me as another member of the faculty, and said, "You be the first director of your group."

Well, I really didn't know a damn thing about it, but the plan was, if you had three cameras, to do your shooting with two of them and keep your third for the possibility that one of the other two would break down.

Well, I thought, this is not a very efficient way to go about this. So I used all the cameras; planned all the shots, the floor positions and so on; and got through that first little scene all right. It came quite easily to me since I was trained in the theatre and had already worked on Broadway.

In subsequent weeks, I was a cameraman, I sat at the audio board, I punched up shots—everyone had to be everything in turn. After a few months Harvey moved on to something else, and I began to teach the course.

Anyway, a friend of mine named Mortie Gottlieb had seen one of the plays that I did in summer stock and thought it was pretty good. Mortie, as you know, is now a producer on Broadway and quite a good one. Anyway, at that time, he was a business manager in the theatre, and someone he knew was working for Kenyon and Eckhart, one of the big Madison Avenue advertising agencies, and they told him that they were looking for someone to direct the *Ford Theatre,* which was about to make its debut on television. The *Ford Theatre* was already a big radio show, but now they wanted to do it on television.

So Mortie recommended me to Garth Montgomery, who was the man in charge at Kenyon and Eckhart. He went to see one of my plays and liked what he saw, but then came the big question: What experience have you had in television?

Well, because of that cockamamie introductory course I had taken at the Wing, I was truthfully able to say that I had directed on television.

You've got to remember that no one had too much experience in television in those days. Everybody was making it up as they went along. Anyway, they hired me—why, I'll never know—but they did, and I began my first job as a television director.

I must interrupt to comment on how extraordinarily early this winter of 1947–1948 was in television's development. In spite of its accelerated growth, television programming as we know and recognize it today really didn't begin to emerge until the spring and summer of 1948 with the presentation of such programs as *The Milton Berle Show, Studio One,* and *Talk of the Town.* Daniels was a true pioneer.

We rehearsed in this great barn of a place called Caravan Hall, on East Fifty-Ninth Street. All the executives from Kenyon and Eckhart, including Garth Montgomery, the head of the Radio and Television Department, decided that they wanted to see a run-through before we went into the studio, so I had some chairs placed for them in the rehearsal hall. The first thing Montgomery asked, when he came in, was "Where's the booth?" That was what he knew from radio—a client's booth. He thought that we had the cameras and everything in the rehearsal hall—I had to tell him that there weren't any. That's how unfamiliar they were with the process. Anyway, they sat through that first rehearsal, and I think they were pleased.

When we finally moved our production out of the rehearsal hall, we went to work at the top of Grand Central Station, where CBS had their studios, in what was called Studio 41, and which later became the studio for *Studio One.* They were building the studio around us as we were rehearsing, driving the actors crazy. No kidding, the carpenters were hammering as we were trying to do our scenes. It was impossible, but we did it just the same. The control room was a kind of plywood box filled with field equipment, which, at that point in time, meant that the studio monitors were only about five by seven inches in size—you really couldn't see much.

I was generally going out of my mind, even though I recall that I was very well prepared—it was a big, complicated deal. I had every shot laid out, marked in the script, with the T.D. sitting next to me on my right, and the A.D. on my left setting up the shots. In spite of my preparation, I didn't know where I was or what I was doing. Remember, all of this was going to be broadcast live. That first *Ford Theatre* was really something.

What can I say? The show got on,* and it wasn't too awful. Everyone seemed to like it, so we continued doing them.

Marc continued to tell me more about those early studio days. The huge, oversized cameras and turret lenses were often unwieldy, limiting movement. Yet, as he said, "The show got on. . . . "

I blocked my shows, and I never worried too much about what lens I was using. I usually let the cameraman decide, and then if my shot was too loose, I'd say, "Use a tighter lens," or if I was too tight, I'd say, "Can you back up?" I was generally too busy to take the time to figure it all out, and besides, it was just a small matter of adjustment, to find out which move was better, taking the camera closer or using another lens. The cameramen were just great, extremely able when it came to using those lenses and flipping them.

I can remember a production of *Light Up the Sky* that we did, starring Sam Levine, who was just about to make his entrance. I wanted to bring him in fairly loose, so that you could see that side of the room, where he was coming from. So he walked in the door, on cue, and said his line, which I don't remember, but, for some reason I've never forgotten the next line by a second character in the room, who said, "And it went off, too." Well, during the two seconds it took to say that line, when I was on the reverse, the cameraman brought Sam in the door, flipped his lens to a close-up, and refocused. The cameramen were incredible—really very, very able.

Technique, as we know it today, was still being shaped by these early directors. It all sounds simple as we describe it now, but those basics still apply and, when forgotten, lead to confusion and chaos on the screen. I asked Marc if there were any principles and techniques that were learned in those first programs that he felt still applied in his work today.

Most of what I do is reflex by this time. But the first thing I learned from Marlowe and still remember is that television is a close-up medium, so whenever I'm on the set or on location, that's the first thing I do—let the audience know where they are, where the people are, and who they are. I always try and follow some kind of establishing procedure. This doesn't mean that it always has to be an establishing shot, especially if you

*The first *Ford Theatre* was a production of Ruth Gordon's play, *Years Ago,* and starred Raymond Massey and Eva La Gallienne. I believe it was broadcast on October 17, 1948.

want a particular effect, like when you begin the scene with a close-up because you don't want the audience to know where they really are.

Films always have establishing shots, but in television you need a close-up as quickly as you can manage one—what I'd call an identifying close-up. Once I've got that, then I can lay back and do almost anything that I want. I'm always surprised at how many directors don't do that. I think it must be very annoying for the audience.

If you're directing a play for the stage, to someone sitting in the audience, you have what might be called an equality ratio. The person in the audience and the person on the stage are life-size to each other, unless, of course, you are sitting in the back of the second balcony. So I usually keep things fairly life-size on stage, just as long as everyone's heard. In film, feature films, you've got that huge screen, where people are larger than life. Therefore, what they do doesn't have to be as big as what they might do in the course of their ordinary behavior.

These are not hard and fast rules, just an approach—what you might do, what you have to watch out for.

I came to television direction very late in my career, having begun in radio and moving into television as an associate and then as a staff producer at CBS, where I worked in what was then called "TV's intellectual ghetto," the Sunday morning programming. It was not until long after I had left the network and started freelancing that I became a hyphenate—a producer-director—and began doing my own direction. Only on special occasions, when I felt I was in over my head technically, did I go out and hire a director for the projects that I was producing. One of the people that I called on in several random instances, when he was available, was Marc. Now, I consider myself a technical incompetent, hardly knowing which way to turn a screwdriver when putting a screw in the wall, so I was a bit surprised to discover that he knew even less about the insides of a camera than I did. I asked him how he could have worked in television for forty years and know nothing technically.

Easily, I guess, (laughs) . . . technical change happens so rapidly in our business; there are so many different kinds of cameras, and tubes, and this, that and the other thing, that I have never wanted to bother with it. That isn't my business; I don't operate the cameras. The only time that I have to worry about them is when someone tells me that it's too hot in the studio and we can't operate the cameras, or that we're in "down" time, and something isn't functioning—but I'm not about to fix it.

My contribution is to put on the show; there are a lot of people in the studio whose sole interest is the technical side of things. I don't want to dissipate what my interests are—what the shots are telling me, what the shots are telling the audience, what the performances are like, all of which I have worked on before we ever got to the studio and the cameras. That's what I do—I'm not the technical director, nor am I a maintenance man. They take care of that stuff; I do the show.

In the training of students, that is something that has always troubled me: Just how much technical training does an aspiring TV director need? A certain amount is mandated, but up until I began to teach regularly, I would have said a minimal amount.

Now I acutely feel the need for structured technical training as part of TV training. The obvious consideration is that the more students know, the more intelligently they will handle their studio tasks, but, even more, because of network cutbacks, recent television graduates are no longer able to walk into the networks as pages and mail room clerks and quickly move up the executive ladder. Break-in jobs have become harder and harder to find. So I see many of our recent graduates accepting jobs as camera people, editors, even full-blown technicians, as a way of getting into the industry. It has redefined for me what can be described as an entry-level position in television, and I go along with it. But it would disturb me terribly if I looked down the road three, four or five years from now and found some of our graduates, whom we had educated so assiduously, still working in the technical end of things.

Marc Daniels was a rarity, even for his time—he started working at the top. If he had any apprenticeship, it was in the theatre. I was also under the impression that he had a longer career in New York than he did, associating him in my mind with some of the productions during the Golden Age of television, but it turned out that he was in California from 1949 to 1954, one of the first of the New York directors to make the exodus to Hollywood.

I went out to the Coast to do *I Love Lucy,* and there's a story to that. Desi and Lucy wanted to move to New York to do the show. As you know, the country was not interconnected as yet, and they wanted the show to be in the most populous part of the country—live—to get the biggest audience.

But they settled against making the move; they felt that it would be too disruptive. The whole reason that they wanted to do the series in the first place was so that they could all be together—they had one child at that point.

So they decided to stay in California, and Desi didn't want to feed bad kinescopes back to the East Coast. They wanted to do the show with multiple film cameras, using them the way that TV would.

An interesting sidelight is that in order to get the network to agree to their plan, they had to put up some of their own money. The cost of doing it their way added twenty thousand dollars to the price of each episode, so they paid for the difference out of their own pocket, and with it, they got a 50-percent interest in the show. Needless to say, they became multimillionaires.

I got involved because I had been in live television and knew how to handle multiple cameras. I knew almost nothing about film at the time, but I had a quick course in what I had to know. They made it easy for me—not too different from what I had known in live TV. They even developed a three-headed movieola for editing which worked like the three monitors in the control room.

It was a very complicated system when we started. Desi's notion, in spite of the fact that we were filming, was to give the studio audience the idea that they were watching a live show, and thereby generate more laughter on the sound track.

So, in the beginning, we tried not to interrupt the continuity of the two acts. We did this by having four synched cameras, and the writers would write up to the limit of each camera's magazine, which meant about ten minutes of running time.

I was up in the booth, not because I was calling shots or anything like that, but just to keep everything going. I had a footage counter for each camera, which would tell me when we would have to reload. We started the show with three cameras, remember we had four, and as each counter would run down, we knew that we would have to reload. Then the craziness began—we would start our fourth camera, stop the one that needed reloading, reload it, break off another that needed reloading, start another, reload, start, reload. As you can imagine, it was an enormously complicated thing—a bit like Russian roulette.

After the first show, which the audience enjoyed tremendously, we had this meeting, and everyone said, "There is just no way we can do this. It's so complicated, and besides it's very expensive—all this wasted raw stock with the cameras running all the time." And the studio floor is so crowded. They had four Fearless dollies, four camera operators, four camera assistants, two booms, two boom pushers, two boom operators. It was a mess.

So I said, "There's an easy way to simplify matters, and that is if we can stop between scenes. Then we can reload without pressure when we have to, and I can use three cameras." So they allowed that that was a good idea. It turned out that it was an even better one from the creative point of view because it meant that you could write scenes where you could change wardrobe, where you could have time lapses, make elaborate makeup changes if you wanted to. For instance, there was one marvelous show where Lucy gets caught in a freezer and comes out with frost all over her, and the only way that it could be done was with a complicated makeup change. You couldn't have done that without a camera break.

Anyway, after the change, the show really took off. They could do much wilder things—and they did. Filming became more and more flexible. If you needed an additional shot of any kind, why you would just do a pickup. I did the show for the whole first season, thirty-eight of them.

Marc was very reluctant to tell me more, saying almost nothing about his separation from the *Lucy* show after that first year of production. He shrugged my questions off with, "Well, we had a few personality conflicts. They weren't the easiest people to work with that first year, but I guess I wasn't either."

Marc moved on after those early *Lucy* shows to another sitcom, *I Married Joan* with Joan Davis, but very early in his career refused to be categorized as someone who only does sitcoms. He developed what has proved to be one of television's more interesting and eclectic careers. He's done all kinds of things: *Bonanza, Gunsmoke, Hogan's Heroes, Star Trek.* He also had an especially long run with Robert Young as *Marcus Welby, M.D.,* even directing some of Young's first ventures in the world of commercials. More prestigiously, he's even directed Sir Lawrence Olivier in a powerful presentation of Graham Greene's *The Power and the Glory.* As he told me, "I'm a director, I direct everything!"

Professionally, our paths had recrossed when Marc had come east and was directing on *The Play of the Week,* of which I was one of the producers. He didn't work for me, but watching him in the studio, I quickly became one of his coterie of admirers. But it was a number of years before we had the opportunity to work together. I was producing for the Westinghouse Broadcasting Company, and we had a project which I thought would benefit from Marc's diplomatic and professional touch.

I remember it well. *The Advocate* was a different kind of directorial stint because I didn't direct the play—all I had to concern myself with were the physical elements that I had to restage for the camera. I didn't have to build any performances. Howard da Silva, who directed for the theatre, did that, and the performances were there—and were very good.

Before we proceed, it might be interesting to clarify this complex project a bit. Westinghouse had taken an option on a Broadway play, securing its reproduction rights, with the idea of letting the play open simultaneously on Broadway and on their owned and operated stations (and on as many other stations that they could sell—stations willing to cancel a whole night of programming to broadcast a play). The project was called *Opening Night on Broadway,* and *The Advocate* was to be the first in a series of such presentations. These reproduction rights are often difficult to negotiate because in the purchase, you are nullifying any further movie or television rights. But *The Advocate* was a difficult and controversial play, and the play's producers, Billy Hammerstein and Michael Ellis, were having trouble raising their production money, so the sale to Westinghouse was made. I was the TV producer.

The Advocate was a play about Sacco and Vanzetti, the Italian anarchists, and their sensational trial. It starred James Daly, a really splendid actor, who has since died and is now known primarily as the father of Tyne Daly of *Cagney and Lacey* fame.

In consultation with the theatrical producers, it was decided to rehearse the play for three weeks under a stock contract, open it in a theatre on Long Island, play it for a week, then close it after its short run and give it over to us for television. We would do whatever would be necessary to make the television transformation and tape the show, and when we were through, Hammerstein and Ellis would redirect the show for the proscenium under a Broadway contract and open it in New York simultaneously with the show we had taped. It was an exciting idea, and the press and the public responded to it.

Marc had been hired to stage the play for the camera's eye. He went on to tell me just what it took to transfer that production from the theatre to the home viewer.

The key to Howard's staging was that he used the center of the stage for what he called "the well of controversy." I remember him discussing it in rehearsal, which I was allowed to sit in on. For him, the action always got down in that "well" center stage, and that was where most of his dramatic confrontations took place.

That was a fine idea, one that worked splendidly for the theatre, but since I had unlimited movement with my cameras and could go wherever I wanted to, I could have confrontations almost anywhere that I decided I wanted them. So I just attacked the play pretty much as I would any other television drama. I made my own choices, and restaged.

I can't remember how many days of rehearsal we had for television before we taped, but I know that it was quite a luxurious amount of time, even though the play was over two hours long. After all, I didn't have to build any performances; they were all there. After rehearsing for three weeks, and then playing it for a week in Mineola, the actors were all well prepared with their roles.

On Broadway, the play failed to gain the respect of the theatre critics, opening and closing on the same night. Paradoxically, the television production of *The Advocate* was almost universally praised in the fifty cities where it eventually played. I asked Marc if he had any theories why this happened. Was it the same play for Broadway that it was for television?

I don't think so. We had advantages on television that they didn't have on Broadway. We could keep the play going; we could build on the impact of it. They were bound by certain physical limitations—not only Howard's "well," but it was a fragmented play, and they were in the position of having to make frequent set changes. They would periodically dim the lights, do some rearranging in the dark, then get the play going again. As I said, it was a very episodic play, a lot of little scenes. They dissipated the audience's attention through the physical limitations of the play.

In television, we didn't have that problem. We could go from one scene to another without losing the audience for even a fraction of a second.

I think this was Marc Daniel's greatest strength—that he was well schooled in the theatre, knew actors and how they achieved performance, knew and recognized excellence in dramatic writing. These things stood him in good stead, whether he was doing *Lucy* or *The Power and the Glory*. At work on *The Advocate,* watching someone else's staging, I could see that he understood every aspect of the process, what it took to change a play into a television show. I asked him if he felt that he could have made the play work for the stage as well as it did for television.

I might have—I don't know. It's a different ball game. I don't know if I could have done it better, but I might have approached it a bit differently. I've always felt and tried to do something in my work which doesn't seem to concern a lot of other people, something I learned when I first started to study acting at the American Academy of Dramatic Arts. That was 1934, and my teacher was a man by the name of Charles Gellinger. He lectured to us frequently about our responsibilities as actors, which I have always felt are the same as our responsibilities as directors.

He told us, when the audience first comes into the theatre, you start off even with them. In order to stay ahead of them, you have to be constantly and continuously interesting. Stay ahead of them, keep their interest; otherwise, they'll get bored, and you'll lose them. That doesn't mean that you have to be constantly and continuously in motion; there are lots of other ways in which you can keep their interest.

In television, it's even more important because all the viewer has to do is push the remote control button and you are gone. So you have to stay ahead of your TV audience, too. And many directors figure, "The hell with them; I'm going to do it my way," imposing all kinds of things on their shows. I can't tell you specifically what I would have done, but I am always aware, in every scene I do, of the audience's response.

A number of years after *The Advocate,* I had the opportunity to call on Marc Daniels again. This was in the waning days of NET, the Ford Foundation–supported production arm of educational television, where I was then a staff producer.

Marya Mannes, the social critic, had written a piece of science fiction called *They,** in which, in her own unique way, she wrote about a society in the future in which the old would be scrupulously "eliminated," except for a few selected writers and artists. It captured some of the arrogance and self-indulgence of the baby boomers, giving a dim view of what they would become as adults. I read it and thought it would make a powerful TV show. Through NET, I negotiated for the rights and subsequently encouraged Marya to write the script. The play was a huge success, mainly because of Marc's visual concepts and direction. Jack Gould of the *New York Times* said it was "directed with masterly sensitivity by Marc Daniels."†

We shot the show all on location in a great old house on Long Island, where six of the artists had been "relocated" by the youth culture. The show was unique on any number of counts, and I asked Marc to share some of his memories of that shoot.

That was an incredible experience, and we did a number of things that up until that time very few TV shows had done. We had a lot of hand-held shots and moved around the beach with our camera, in and around the rooms of that great old house. If you remember, we even borrowed a cherry-picker from the phone company and shot off the tip of that thing.

Most television dramas up until then had used multiple cameras, switching between them, even on location. We used a single videotape camera like a film camera, and that might have been a first.

*Marya Mannes, *They* (Garden City, N.Y.: Doubleday & Co., 1968).
†Jack Gould, " 'They' Adapted as Haunting TV Drama," *New York Times,* April 18, 1970.

It was a little difficult to organize, but we stayed pretty close to script, went scene to scene, didn't shoot out of continuity. We didn't have to, everything we shot was in one basic location, in and around the house. The only reason you go out of continuity is when you want to do all the scenes that occur in a certain set at the same time.

Incidentally, I used a production board on that show, which was something that had been used in Hollywood for a long time with film, but I think this was the first time it had ever been used on a tape shoot. It worked out fine, and I've used one many times since.

Very simply, it allows for the organization of your show, all of its scenes, onto strips of various colors, in which each strip has everything on it that's relevant in that scene: the cast, where the scene takes place, what they're wearing, whether it's day or night, are there any extras—that sort of detail. These strips are placed on a board and can be moved around—grouped in any way you want. And, of course, the best thing about the board is that every time you finish a scene, you can remove the strip and put it aside. In a glance, then, you have a wonderful sense of the progress you are making on your shoot, what you still have left to do.

You usually shoot out of continuity for economic reasons. You don't want to go back to the same location a dozen times, if it's not necessary. It's much better for performers when you don't because when you keep your line of continuity, it gives them a chance to develop their characters, their performances.

Because Marc is a director who is equally at home with film or videotape, I asked him if he were given a choice at the start of production, which one he would choose.

It depends on the kind of production you're doing, and there are all kinds of options now. I still enjoy working on multicamera tape productions, mainly because the chances are that you are going to get the opportunity to rehearse a bit more. And I always feel that the more that you can rehearse, the better you can make it. Most of the situation comedies that are played in front of audiences here in California are rehearsed. You have three or four days of rehearsal before the audience comes in. But then, on the other hand, there's something like *M*A*S*H*—that's a sitcom that was done without rehearsal. It was shot on film. They'd run the scene several times just to set movement, and then they'd shoot it, and no one can quarrel with the results of *M*A*S*H*.

But rehearsal, to my way of thinking, is always better. In the early days of *Lucy*, everybody used to say how spontaneous the show was. Well, it was spontaneous because it was so well rehearsed. The actors became so familiar with what they were going to be called upon to do that it completely freed them, and they could really enjoy what they were performing.

But I don't think I really have a preference; I like to work in both mediums. Today you can do almost anything you want whether it's film or tape, and both have their strengths. If you are shooting a single tape camera, the look is indistinguishable from film. Tape cameras can do anything that film cameras can. And in the editing process, even film is being transferred to tape for editing nowadays. Tape editing is a lot simpler and easier than film editing. For one thing, you can see your image immediately. If you want a dissolve, you just do it in the editing. You don't have to send it to the optical house, get it back, decide you don't like it and have to send it back again.

About the only time that I really prefer working on film is when you are doing something outdoors—in rugged terrain, things of that nature—where the physical problems are somewhat acute. On location, you can have twenty problems with your cable before you can even get your first shot. Then I prefer film because television cameras have too many things that can go wrong with them, and a film camera is a fairly simple mechanism.

It was getting late, and I had promised Marc that I wouldn't keep him from his daily swim, which I was to discover consisted of a hundred lengths, a mile a day. Marc had suffered a heart attack some years before and had recovered, but now was addicted to this daily regimen. Most directors I know rely very heavily on some kind of physical conditioning. Studio days can be long and trying; studio floors are usually poured concrete and can kill your arches. Days on location can also be fatiguing. Whatever the situation, if you want to be a director, you need to remain in good health, have a clear mind and have the ability to sustain long and arduous shoots in relatively good humor.

But there were still things I wanted to ask him, and I pushed for more time. I wondered about post-production and just how involved he got once his shoots were finished.

It depends on what the project is. The Director's Guild agreement with the producers says that you must be involved in post-production. In fact, you have the right to the first cut of any show you make. But in episodic television—doing an hour show, for example—there's no way you can hang in there, by mutual agreement. Once you have finished shooting, you are usually going on to another shoot, maybe another episode of the same show, and it may take two or three weeks for the edit to be finished. Besides, it's usually pretty much of a routine matter, especially if the show staff has good production notes.

I then asked Marc if he had a television style that's uniquely his—something that he imposes on every show that he directs.

I don't really think so, although a lot of people have told me that they could tell a show of mine, even before they saw the credits. I've asked them what they saw, but they were not able to pin anything specific down. I know that I said something to you before about establishing where people are and who they are, getting to identify them quickly. But I don't think that's enough to impose a unique style on a show. I really don't know myself what I do. It's just that whatever it is, I keep on doing it.

I was curious whether he ever tried to make pretty pictures. In other words, I wondered if there were any aesthetic principles that he applied to his work.

Certainly, I think everyone wants to make pretty pictures all of the time. You want good composition for your shots; you want beautiful color, well-matched cameras and so on. But a lot of your ability to get what you want out of a situation depends on the situation. Most of the time, in television, you're in and out of the studio so quickly, you don't have much time for aesthetics—but that's no reason not to try.

Pre-production can be terribly important for a director in setting the look of his show. I try and talk up the look I want well before I've gotten my first shot. I talk to my cameramen, my lighting guy, the scenic designer, of course—anyone and everyone who is going to contribute to the look of my show in some way. And they all contribute, making suggestions that I will go along with, knowing the show will look better because of it. You can't stop production in the middle of a shoot and say, "Now, I want a pretty picture here." It just happens as you proceed and becomes part of the story you are telling.

I also asked about using personnel in the studio. He's a lovely man, a nice guy, and I wondered what happened when he had to push someone around.

Well, if I have to push, I push. I think a director should know enough about what everyone does to be able to let that person do his job and, when they don't, to be able to gently remind them that they are not. There are directors who don't know enough about the workings of a set to be able to function effectively, so they start pushing. I like to give everyone a chance to do their job, and I expect them to do the same for me.

So, for example, I'm very impatient about noise on the set, especially when I feel it's distracting to the actors. I'm also quite strict about having the set quiet when the technicians are working, trying to communicate with each other. I think you have to give people a chance to do their work.

I had only one last question: You've had a long and full career; you've done everything. What's still left to do? Do you have any strong feelings about what you'd like to see in the way of work in these next couple of years?

Every type of thing that you do has its advantages and its disadvantages. I'd like to make another feature film, for example. I did one once in Australia for GROUP W that didn't work quite as well as I wanted it to, and I'd like to try that again. But if you do a feature, you often spend two years of your life on it, and it all comes to naught.

Then, too, I'd like to do a play on Broadway. Work in the theatre has many wonderful advantages, like working in front of an audience, which is a great privilege. But, there again, you can work for six months or a year on a play, and it opens and closes in two nights.

With television, at least, you don't spend all that much time. If a show is successful, that's wonderful; if it isn't, it doesn't matter all that much because you go on to another one in a matter of weeks.

I really don't know what I would like to do. I'd just like to keep working—whatever it is, I'm interested.

5

Don Mischer: Directing at the Kennedy Center

Television came to San Antonio, Texas, where Don Mischer was born, in 1949. He was eight years old at the time, but says that he remembers being "knocked off my feet by that thing in which pictures travel through the air." Don obviously never forgot those early TV images, but it was to be many years before he would recognize the great impact that those early black-and-white shows would have on him.

A tall, angular man with glasses, Mischer looks like someone who would wear a pair of cowboy boots with his tuxedo and leave his Stetson at the Kennedy Center checkroom before he shot his show there. One of the brightest men I have ever met in a control room, he's a paradox in the fast-talking, glitzy world of show business.

Mischer was initially discouraged by his parents from pursuing a career in show business and instead followed what he describes as a "natural aptitude for math" into a course of study in sociology and political science. He did his undergraduate and graduate work at the University of Texas in Austin. He had completed his master's degree and was publishing papers in obscure academic journals like the *Southwestern Social Science Quarterly*, about to get his Ph.D. in sociology, when the most dramatic event of his generation took place. It changed Don forever.

I was also interested in national politics, and on a Friday afternoon, John Kennedy was due to make an appearance in Austin, Texas. This was November 22, 1963. He was coming from Dallas, and, of course, on his way to the airport, he was shot and died. I was part of a delegation that was to go to the airport and meet him, and when we heard the news, you

Don Mischer (Photo courtesy of Bob Marshak.)

can just imagine, we were in a state of shock. I mean, unbelievable grief, and guilt that it had happened in the state of Texas. So there we all were, at the airport, completely thrown off our feet.

Well, in a matter of hours all these television people came down from New York. Lyndon Johnson was now president, and everyone wanted to do stories about him. What about his background? What about his ranch? What about his days in the Texas legislature? What are the other influences on his life?

I knew a lot about Lyndon Johnson because I had studied political science. So a few of us got connected through the political science department at the university with these producers, and over that weekend, when we were feeling those highly personal feelings, we threw ourselves into what we were doing.

I was simply knocked out by what I saw, impressed by these able people who came down from New York and did stories, which, within a matter of two or three hours, forty or fifty million people would be seeing on network television. And I said, "This is really what I want to do; this is where it's at."

In the following year, the Ford Foundation gave out ten grants to encourage people in other academic disciplines to learn about television, and I got one of those. The grant was worth something like twenty-six hundred dollars a year, which enabled me to start work at the public television station in Austin. When I started to work there, I pulled cables, worked in the scenic shop, learned to run tape machines and cameras, and by the end of that year, I was already doing some directing.

That sounded a long way from the very heady scene of directing variety shows in Hollywood, and I wanted to know how he made that transition. What had he discovered in the course of that Ford Foundation year that prepared him for the kind of work that he was now doing?

More than anything, I learned about myself, that I had a sense of visual things, an aptitude toward music, a good idea of what worked in television and what didn't. I learned about the craft of television: I learned the basic skills in that year, and I learned them under the best possible conditions.

I feel compassion for the young people who call me up here in the office every week—I get no less than fifteen calls a week—and ask, "What can I do to get going? I want to learn about television. Where can I go?" And there is no place; there are no opportunities like the one that I had.

We were sitting in the large, comfortable offices of Don's production company, on Wilshire Boulevard, in Beverly Hills, surrounded by the artifacts of his success, and it seemed incongruous to be talking about break-in jobs and his first few early assignments in public television. I wanted to bring him into his current career with *its* problems and attainments. I refreshed his memory about the first time we had met in the offices of NET in New York, and he recalled.

I was working for Channel 9 in Austin, KLRN–TV, part of the educational television network, and I was doing an accounting show called *Strictly Business*. It was kind of a poor man's *Wall Street Week*, and I met a guy in Austin named Ronnie Dugger who published a paper called the *Texas Observer*. It was a liberal paper, a thorn in the side of Texas politics, and this guy was incredible. He would go out and dig up these stories of corruption and create waves that would shudder the establishment down there.

Well, we started doing little pieces with Dugger for television and shipped them up to NET in New York. Al Perlmutter was doing something at the time called *At Issue*, which was a weekly, one-hour, all-on-location series of short documentaries, and he started to use the pieces: a ten-minute piece of shenanigans being played out in the Texas legislature about state contracts that looked a bit peculiar, a ten-minute bit about oyster beds that were being fouled by sewage—that kind of thing. . . . Dugger would do most of the content work, dig up the stories, and I would produce and direct the stuff for television.

About the same time, I started doing music shows in Austin. It was an incredible place—every night we did two to six live shows. On Wednesday night, for example, we would start in Studio A with a live show from six to seven, then the crew would switch over to Studio B for a half-hour live show and during that time some of us would be changing A over so that we could come back at nine o'clock for a one-hour live music special.

I had opportunities to direct that were unbelievable, and the shows I didn't direct I would run camera on. We did *Tosca*, the entire opera, with the Austin and the University of Texas opera companies on two black-and-white cameras, and I ran one of them. I would run camera for my peers who would be directing, and then they would run them for me when I would direct. I got to do the Houston Symphony Orchestra with John Barbaroli conducting, as a cameraman. Everything happened quickly, and we did a lot of mediocre shows, but we were out there trying. The money at the station was not going into equipment or fancy offices, but was right up there on the screen where it counted.

I asked what finally brought him to New York?

I actually went from Texas to Washington first. I worked for the USIA, doing propaganda shows about America. I would do shows about American music: what's happening in Motown, what's happening with the Beach Boys. Shows about American artists, about American fashion, the new fall line, that kind of thing. Gentle propaganda about the American scene, which was then shown in countries overseas.

I worked with Charles Guggenheim, a brilliant film maker, whom I learned a tremendous amount from. I did some political things for him. I produced a spot campaign for Teddy Kennedy, who was running for Congress in Massachusetts.

But then Al Perlmutter called me and said, "Come to New York and direct a show we're going to produce called *The Great American Dream Machine*." At that time, I was committed to being a free-lancer in Washington, doing my own things, but Al's call changed all that. I went to New York, did the *Dream Machine*, and after that, things opened up for me in New York, until I decided to come out here about ten years ago.

About three years after *Dream Machine* ended its run on NET—and NET was closing up shop, swallowed up by the new Public Broadcasting System—I had been hired by a production company formed by the comic Alan King and a partner, Rupert Hitzig, to produce a telethon for the United Jewish Appeal in New York City, and King–Hitzig Productions told me that they had also hired Don Mischer to direct for them. Telethons are long and complicated assignments, and I was delighted to hear that Don would be part of the show. I had enough to do putting the six-hour show together; I didn't want to worry about getting the show on and off the air.

The broadcast was a huge success. We raised more money for charity in New York City at that one show that had ever been raised before using a telethon format. Better still, the long and difficult program ran without a hitch. I was to become a fan of Don's forever. King–Hitzig also became devoted admirers of Mischer's work, and when they were given an assignment to become the executive producers of a new Howard Cosell variety show, they turned to Don Mischer as their director. I discussed his budding New York career with him, as well as some of the conflicts engendered by that Cosell show.

When you do good work, and you treat people well, it always comes back to help you. When the *Dream Machine* broke up, after it had completed its run, everyone went their different ways, and I began to get a lot of work from some of the people I had worked with. I did some industrial things for the state of New York, I worked for the Children's Television Workshop, did some *Electric Company*'s, got involved in one of their pilot series, *Feeling Good*. Bob Shanks, who had produced some segments for

Dream Machine, went over to ABC and was put in charge of late night television, and I did a "rock and roll" show for him. It was called *In Concert*, and it was on Friday nights at 11:30. I had fun doing that.

That spring, there were two big new shows that were going to be offered out of New York on network television. One was *The Howard Cosell Show*. Prime time, Saturday night, big press and promotion, live, produced by Roone Arledge of ABC Sports; executive producer, Alan King. They had plans to replicate the success of *The Ed Sullivan Show*, and it sounded great, besides offering me a very attractive deal financially, so I accepted.

The other show was being produced by a young guy who I felt was pretty much unproven. He had been a writer on *Laugh-In*, and though I liked him very much, and he was exceedingly bright, I thought it was a very chancy show. I felt that he was going to have a hard time succeeding; there were going to be a lot of network obstacles to overcome. Well, of course, that producer's name was Lorne Michaels, and that show was *Saturday Night Live*.

I had done a lot of late night television by that time, and although I knew that *Saturday Night Live* had a good chance to become a very "in" show, I never dreamed that it would become as successful as it did. I chose to take the longer commitment and the prime time slot, but it was a mistake—in hindsight.

But if I had to do it over again, I would probably make the same decision, but you have to admit I had my nose rubbed in it somewhat. About one year after Howard Cosell went off the air, there I was looking at *Saturday Night Live* collecting all the Emmies, and it rankled.

The Cosell show obviously didn't slow Mischer's career. A good director, especially a good variety director like Mischer, has skills which are useable and saleable to producers. If you will note, Don always speaks positively about his experiences, and if there is blame to be laid, he puts it on himself. It's a good lesson to learn—never to bad-mouth a project you are, or have been, involved in. There are friends and critics aplenty who are more than willing to do that for you.

Keep a high regard for your own work, for if you don't, no one else will. That doesn't mean being unduly arrogant, or unrealistic about what you have done, but students especially have a tendency to undermine their own programs in the course of production. My advice is to step back from the show if you can. Take a brief respite and then relook at what you have done. It will always look better than you think it did.

In spite of Cosell, Don's career continued to flourish, even more so when he decided to go to Hollywood. I asked him why he went.

My goal was always to be at the top of my field, directing and producing variety, music, dancing programs—that's what I liked the most. It became obvious after spending four or five years in New York that it was very hard to do those kind of things there. New York was the production center for news, for sports, and for some soaps, but all the entertainment stuff was being done in California. The last two years that I lived in New York, I spent more than half of my time on the Coast, commuting back and forth.

. . .

Anyway, it finally became obvious that I would have to make the move. Gary Nardino, who was my agent at the time, set up a meeting for me with George Schlatter who was planning a revival of *Laugh-In*, and we hit it off. George made me a definite commitment, so out I came, and we did seven, not terribly successful revivals of that show. But you can't say that it was a total failure because we did discover Robin Williams and a few other people in the process.

Laugh-In provided the base for me, and I went on from there. I did a John Denver special with George, then a Goldie Hawn special, and by then, I was being asked to participate in a lot of interesting projects.

And he has. I don't think there's a project in Hollywood that involves variety entertainment that Don Mischer isn't considered for, at the very least. He's even returned to New York in the last couple of years to successfully produce and direct the Tony Awards show, the annual presentation of awards for excellence in the theatre. Almost everything that Don does boggles the imagination, has tremendous magnitude to it. I asked him how he managed to keep his eye on content when every show that he did got to be as big as a three-ring circus.

That's the biggest problem with television direction, I think. You have to be aware of, be conscious of, keep one's eye on what is going on physically—and still concentrate on content.

When you're in the control room with your headset on, in one ear, the lighting director is trying to talk to you; in the other, the audio guy has got a problem; the stage manager tells you that they can't get the scenery to fly in right, et cetera, et cetera, et cetera. You're trying to watch the shot: the hair is not quite right, there is something wrong under her right eye. Finally the realities of what you are doing catch up with you: Is this scene funny? Is this emotional moment working the way that it should? Is there anything that I can do to make this better, more powerful? Most of all, if it's not working—why isn't it?

I think it's the main problem with being a producer and director on the same show: you sometimes miss the obvious. What I have done with the people that I now have around me is to try and delegate certain responsibilities in certain areas, so that I am freer to concentrate on content, because in the end it's what is happening on the screen in terms of its total impact that makes something work or not. And you can really get thrown off if you are bogged down in technical areas. Yet, paradoxically, it's my familiarity with what the camera can do, and my familiarity with the lights and the moods that can be established using filters, that kind of thing, that enables me to do some of the kinds of things I do that are successful.

In most of my projects now, when I'm wearing two hats, I normally have a partner, and I stay heavily involved in producing until a few days before we tape the event; when we start going full blast, then I become the director. I sometimes have to make a decision or two about an artist or something in the middle of the taping, but my head and my energy are in directing—you can't do it any other way.

On *Motown 25*, the Motown twenty-fifth anniversary show, Suzanne De Passe was the executive producer, and I co-produced it with Buzz Kohan. He wrote it, I directed it, and we all worked together, producing, until the last week, when I focused on the direction of the show. There was no way I could do it otherwise.

Let me give you an example. Richard Pryor was the host, okay. Before the taping, I had several meetings at Pryor's house with Buzz and Suzanne, and we laid out the show, what he was going to do. Now everything's set, but in the last hours before the show when I'm rehearsing with the Temptations and the Four Tops on the stage, what do I say if Pryor comes up to me an hour before he's supposed to go and says, "I don't like this speech in which I introduce the Jackson Five." Well, I just couldn't stop what I was doing to make a rewrite, so Buzz and Suzanne addressed themselves to it, and that worked out real well—it's nice to have compatible people to work with.

As the industry changes, I see more and more hyphenates on the credits. "Produced and directed by" has become a commonplace appellation. Don Mischer, as he tells us, has obviously developed a working relationship with his staff and cohorts that allows him to do both of his jobs with equal fluency. I think a common mistake of people who are putting shows together—assembling staffs, assigning roles and functions and, most of all, clarifying their own job on the projected program—is that they don't define the tasks they want their personnel to perform. They hire their friends and acquaintances, who then try to replicate and duplicate each other. A good rule in pre-production is to never hire anyone to perform the function that you intend to devote yourself to; find people to do what you won't, don't or cannot do.

Even though much of Mischer's work nowadays is in the origination and development of projects, Mischer told me that he still liked to direct and, for example, continued to direct the *Kennedy Center Honors*.

It's the only show I continue to direct, without any involvement as a producer. I've done it for eight years because George Stevens, Jr., and Nick Vanoff, who co-produce it, are exceptionally gifted producers, with incredible contacts in both Washington and Hollywood, and they do a great job with it. And besides, it's a show that basically comes together in its last week, and that's a luxury for me, so I just direct, and I love it. Now that I both produce and direct, when I go into a direct-only situation, it's like a breath of fresh air, and just terrific to have the producer's problems off my back.

Almost everything that Don does seems to be a remote of some kind. I asked if he had done this deliberately—stay out of the studio.

Studio stuff is just not working as well as it used to anymore. But there are exceptions. Take the last Shirley MacLaine special that I did; that was all done in the studio. Shirley is wonderful to work with, and it was a terrific show: a very innovative, very creative show, but it didn't get the audience that it should have. For some reason, at this time, people don't seem to be interested in studio-based shows. . . .
Now *Motown 25* was the number one show for the week it was on—okay? It had a sense of event. So the things that I'm doing for the rest of the year are all going to be in that direction. Not that I think that studio-based variety programs are dead, but I do think we've hit a lull. So if I talk to a Barry Manilow now, or a Shirley MacLaine, or Barbara Mandrell, or any of the personalities who have commitments for TV specials—and I have spoken to these people—I'm not interested in doing the show unless we can do something that will maximize our chances for success. I know that going into a studio with a concept and some scenery, and taping eight bars at a time, may look beautiful, be lit beautifully and be perfectly executed, but I know there will be something missing.
I did *Ain't Misbehavin'* for NBC about a year ago, and when we started, the assumption was that we could come in—there were something like 40 odd songs in this big Broadway show—do five, six songs a day, taping over a five-day period. This is the typical variety show approach, and NBC had set it up like that, but when Richard Maltby, who produced the show on Broadway, and I got to thinking about it, we said, "No, let's not do it that way." We told NBC we might have a polished performance, but the show will have no soul, no energy, and I convinced them not to do it that way. We ended up rehearsing for four days and taping it just once in front of

a live audience. We didn't stop, we didn't go back, we didn't do any pickups.

And what happened was that the cast knew this, the cameramen knew this, everybody knew that there was going to be only one time through— live on tape. Everybody got all fired up, just like we were doing a live show, and the cast turned in a performance that was really sensational. Richard Maltby, who also directed the show on Broadway, said that he had never seen a performance like this one. The audience felt like they were at a live event; they loved it and fed energy back to the cast; the cast fed it right back to the audience, and it was a high for everyone.

It was magic, it really worked and I know that if we had done the show in typical variety style, we would have been there until two o'clock in the morning, every night, for five nights in a row, with minimal results. What we got on tape had some imperfections. The camera work was not perfect, for example, and on the audio, all of which was live, mind you—I didn't use a band track on the show—there was an occasional clinker in the band, a note on the saxophone, a drum hit that was off. There were even times that a lyric was botched, but I'll tell you, we had soul, we had energy, we had excitement and the damned thing worked.

Risk taking is an important part of the director's job, and Don felt that it was more important to have the energy that was inherent in that show on the screen, rather than having a perfect production. Making the right decisions is a crucial part of our business, and more experience usually means that you won't make mistakes on the little things that you do, but when you do make a mistake, it will be a beauty: an unworkable script, a major piece of casting that was wrong, an overworked set that draws too much attention. Don obviously got home free on *Ain't Misbehavin'*. It doesn't happen every time, even to the most talented of producers, like Don.

I questioned Don's enthusiasm for working in the field, working live on tape. What was there in studio production that had turned him off?

When you do a scene or a musical number in a studio, there is always a reason to do it again. So many times you sit there as a director and you say, "Okay, I can live with that take," and you check everyone in the studio: lighting says, "That was good for me"; audio says, "That was good for me"; but the guy on the crane says, "There was a hit in the middle of it. There was a bobble. We've got to do it again." So we do it again for the crane, for Camera Two. And now we've got: great for Camera Two, great for lights, no good for audio; we got a pop on his mike when he turned around, did this or that, whatever. When you are in a studio doing a variety show, there is always a reason to do it again, and when you get down to the point where it's good for video, good for audio, good for lighting, good for cameras, good for picture composition, then the dancing isn't right.

By the time you finally get it right, and you look at the tape, the magic isn't there anymore. All of us in the business are always striving for perfection; we keep pushing in that direction, but at what cost? It doesn't happen all the time, too many times what you end up with on the screen is not as good as what you had on the second take.

But I wondered whether that also happens in the field. It strikes me that you have even less control in the field than you have in the studio. There are a thousand more things that can go wrong when you are out on location.

I agree. These things can happen out in the field, too, but the show will have a different look to it. I did a special with Marlo Thomas recently, on ABC, on location, in which we did twenty-six takes before we got the shots we wanted, and we had closed off an entire street in New York. If something isn't right, you just can't let it go.

It all comes down to the same thing, whether you're on location or in a studio. You have to know what you are doing, be very well organized and then maintain control—don't let things get away from you; if you do, you maximize your chances of chaos.

Now, being outside, it's true, there are more things that can go wrong. Trucks can drive by, airplanes fly overhead, the RF mikes don't work, there is static interference or you pick up a radio-controlled taxi on call. Then, of course, you can always have weather problems.

But, of course, what you gain is reality, and that gives you a look that you can't create in the studio. You have real backgrounds, real people, a real feeling, and in the studio—I don't care what you do or what you design—you always have that studio look, and the audience knows the difference. They may not know it in words they can describe, but they can feel it, and it makes for an entirely different show.

As you can guess, I love shooting on location. It's also cheaper, if you know what you are doing. I like to shoot on location with two cameras and two tape machines, each camera slaved to a machine. It's a film-style approach, but in true film style you are shooting with one camera, lighting for that shot. This gets very cumbersome on most tape budgets because if you and I are having a conversation, we light for your close-up, shoot that, then we turn the camera around, light for my close-up and shoot that. It's a slow process and an unwieldy one, especially if you're trying to capture the mood of the place you're in. It becomes so manipulated that we lose any magic that might be happening there. I would rather chance an occasional light shadow in exchange for the spirit of the location.

I asked Don how he used those two cameras on location for a variety show shoot.

Let's take Baryshnikov, for example. I did Mischa on location, in the back lot at Universal, in Studio City. We did a chase around the complete lot, choreographed by Michael Kidd, and the entire thing was shot on two cameras. If Baryshnikov was running around a corner with a bunch of dancers chasing him, I would have one camera down low on the street, on a high hat, lens as low to the ground as possible. Now, that gives me a head-to-toe shot of Mischa running down this block and rounding the corner.

The second camera I'd put high on a building, which gave me a master shot with a sense of the whole back lot, and I'd shoot the two cameras simultaneously, so I don't have to go back and do any retakes.

I don't want any close-ups of Baryshnikov when he's running and dancing down the street. I want to see the full figure. Now, if I suddenly have a scene where he runs up to a girl who is standing by a lamppost, and he stops and says something to her, then I don't need the wide shot—I need to go tight. So I'll keep the one camera on the head-to-toe, and with the other, I'll get a tight two-shot of Mischa and the girl. What I do with my two cameras continually changes depending on what the action is. It saves a lot of setups that way, and you don't have to repeat the same actions over and over again.

How many cameras do you use on your Kennedy Center shots—more than two, I hope?

More than two. The *Kennedy Center Honors* show is a live-on-tape event, and I use nine cameras. I have to be prepared for any contingency. The president is there, all of Washington is there—the cultural and political elite of the country. I can't ever stop the show; I can't even delay to set up something. The most I've ever needed to hold up performance is 10 to 15 seconds. With the political bigwigs and stars like Isaac Stern, Leonard Bernstein, Marilyn Horne, we must proceed quickly and efficiently through the evening, and so, as I said, I cover myself with nine cameras, with four feeds that I'm recording. I'm always doing line cuts. For example, if I'm doing a symphonic piece on the show, I have a complete score and all my shots are marked on that score.

I asked Don how much shooting from the hip he does.

Well, sometimes you find that you have to shoot from the hip. The more preparation that I do, the more familiar I am with the music, the dancing, the dialogue; the more time that I've had to rehearse, the better I am at changing my mind and winging it at the last minute. As you must have guessed by now, I believe in preparation—lots of preparation. But there are some shows, like the *Kennedy Center Honors* and *Motown 25*, where you have no other alternative but to "wing" some segments. On the Kennedy Center show I often have had 60 percent of the show rehearsed, ready to tape on a Sunday night, and then at two o'clock in the afternoon, an entire new act is brought down from New York. "Oh, by the way, the entire cast of *42nd Street* is coming down—they're going to do a number." Those are the times that I have to wing it.

On *Motown 25* we weren't able to rehearse much of that show because many of the Motown artists we didn't even see until they were on stage. For the entire last act, reuniting Diana Ross and the Supremes, we had no run-through, no mike rehearsal, no lighting rehearsal. So you're on a total wing, and it's just gut instinct and experience that pays off for you. And, of course, you protect yourself with isolated feeds, if you have any.

That means that you are creating a lot of your show in post-procduction. When Diana Ross came down the aisle at *Motown*, I had a close-up of her isolated all along because I didn't know when she was going to turn around with that wonderful smile of hers and wave at someone in the audience, or look up at Berry Gordy in his box and wink. You don't know when these things are going to happen, especially if you haven't rehearsed anything.

I wondered if Don remembered any show that he had ever done where everything went off without a hitch, without a glitch.

A perfect show? It's rare. I do remember a couple where I didn't have to wing anything. Bob Hope's 80th birthday show, which I just directed, didn't produce, was one. It was planned as a three-hour show at the Kennedy Center, and Bob was concerned about doing it effectively. We had a meeting about a month before the scheduled show date. Bob had apparently done a number of shows in which, for a two- or three-hour program, they would spend six hours taping. They'd stop, go back and do something over again, and the audience would become terribly restless. It made for a long, tiresome, and not very successful evening, both in the house and on the screen.

Bob was primarily concerned about making the evening work well. All of Washington was going to be there, including President and Mrs. Reagan, and he was very firm about what he wanted: "I don't want to keep those people waiting. I want the evening to start on time and finish on time."

I said, "Bob, if you can let me know three weeks in advance whom you've booked, and if you don't come in at the last minute and make a whole lot of changes, or book a whole lot of new people, throw this song out or add this song, and change the rundown—I can be that organized." But I warned him that it never happens—nobody, but nobody, makes those decisions ahead of time.

But he said, "I'll do it." And true to his word, two-and-a-half weeks before the show, we got a rundown. The show was booked, and it never changed.

I also said, "Bob, there are a few other things I want. I want to bring two stage managers from L.A., I want my two personal assistants to come from L.A., I want an L.A. lighting director, I want an L.A. technical director and I want to bring four of my own cameramen." I fully expected Bob to say, "Forget it, I'm not going to pay for that. That's crazy. There are good guys that you can get in Washington and New York." But he said, "Yes." Once he said that, and once I got the rundown, I knew that I could do what he wanted.

So we did a three-hour show in front of the president celebrating Bob Hope's birthday. We started at 7:30, promptly, at the Kennedy Center—black tie audience all in place. We did the first act, took a twenty-five-minute intermission, and the curtain came down at 10:38. And it was a wonderful evening. Bob felt good, we all felt good and everybody enjoyed the show, especially the President.

Again, as in the case with *Ain't Misbehavin'*, we got momentum going, and when Phyllis Diller walked out there, and Lucille Ball walked out there, and all the other stars—unlike other shows, they felt the excitement; they knew we weren't going to stop in spite of the occasional little mistakes here and there. It was as if they were doing a live show, and as I say, it was terrific.

The telephone was ringing on Don's desk, in spite of the fact that he had left instructions with his secretary that he was not to be disturbed during our conversation. In the call which ensued, I could hear Mischer dealing with some crisis or other in his quiet manner. When he hung up, feeling the pressure, I indicated that I was almost finished. Most of all, I didn't want to leave without asking him about his experiences with Twyla Tharp, the gifted choreographer whom he had collaborated with in his earlier New York days. I had recently viewed the *Twyla Tharp Show* at the Museum of Broadcasting and was struck by how technically innovative it was. I asked him to reminisce a bit about it—the process of collaboration, the show's uniqueness, the planning that must have gone into it:

It was a show that kind of evolved. I had met Twyla Tharp through the work that I had done at Channel 13 in New York, the public television station. At that point in my career I was doing late night rock concerts on ABC, and I was looking for an opportunity to do something different. I wanted something to get my teeth into; I guess I wanted to prove to myself what I thought I was capable of in television.

Television direction is very much a group activity; you are as good as the people around you. You can be the best director in the world, but if you have lousy people on camera, nobody good on lighting for you, then you're struggling, and your work is not going to show. To do a show right, you need time, you need to prepare well and you need good people working with you. I learned that from Dwight Hemion, who in my mind is the best at doing variety work. He surrounds himself with top people and, consequently, does the best work.

I guess at that point in my career I wanted to test myself. I kept saying that I wanted a show where I could really prepare and do some experimental things. Well, nobody had any budget for that kind of program, and if they did, it was minimal. Then the Twyla Tharp thing came along, and I saw that as the opportunity I was waiting for. It was planned as kind of a marriage between a creative artist, Twyla, and television, which was me.

I turned down a couple of other offers that year that would have made me a lot more money, and Twyla turned down $80,000 from the Wolf Trap Foundation for a summer's internship, and instead, we decided to work together. We were both paid a relatively small fee for our efforts, but we both decided that we wanted to do this.

Anyway, it became a real labor of love. I knew from her work, which I had seen at the Brooklyn Academy of Music, that she was a very spirited and innovative lady and that it would be fun to work with her—and it was. We didn't go into the project with any great plan. The money came from the National Endowment for the Arts, and their only request was that while we were working on our collaboration, they wanted a black-and-white documentary crew filming what was going on. And what happened was that the process that we went through became almost more interesting than the show we ended up producing.

We started out wanting to do a dance on television with no dancers, using the computer to generate all our images, but we quickly saw that there wasn't going to be a whole lot there that hadn't been seen before, and that wasn't that exciting. Then we were just going to shoot a whole lot of thumbs and elbows and toes, and see if we could do some "choreography" with that, but that didn't work either. In the end, what we did was not that extraordinary, but what made the show unusual was the process we went through to achieve what we did. It was a mind-blowing experience from start to finish, and I was never sorry for one moment that I did it.

In the *Twyla Tharp Show*, Don was among the first to use some of the new computerized, digitized developments in television. I think of him as a very innovative and creative guy, and now there are all kinds of different things coming on the market. I was curious whether he has any use for them in the kind of commercial things that he does.

I try and stay aware of these changes, and I do use them. Now, every new device that comes along everybody in town uses right away, so that new developments can become clichés very quickly. I find that most people use these things very uncreatively, mainly because someone else is using them, not because they have thought them through and decided what they want to do creatively and why. Your objective should be to make what you are doing on television—new innovation or not—work.

In my opinion, if you have what I call a "magic moment" occurring on the screen—a great singer, a great dance number—you do not have to cut excessively or manipulate the video. At the end of the last Shirley MacLaine special, she did a little direct-to-camera talk about what she wanted the world to be like, and then she did a special arrangement of John Lennon's *Imagine*. I've forgotten the exact lyrics—"Imagine if we were all at peace, and there were no wars," and all that. The song was about three-and-a-half minutes long. I took a look at it the first time it was on camera, and I had some great shots planned. I wanted to start tight and then come back to a very wide shot. I had a Titan Crane that went up 45 feet in the air. Once I made my move, I had plans to super her head tight over this wide shot. I had all the moves planned, all of which were quite tasteful and worked.

Anyway, when I saw Shirley perform the song, I said, "I don't dare change the camera on this lady. What she is creating with her performance and her attitude and her music, the look in her eyes, the overall effect— why, it sends goose bumps up and down my spine. It's so wonderfully gentle, so emotional, it's going to have people in tears." So, instead, I did it in one simple shot. I started on a medium shot and very, very slowly moved into a head shot, and it turned out to be one of the most dramatic pieces of tape I've ever seen. I didn't cut, I didn't show off, I didn't do any zingy things from my end and it was perfect.

Now, if you have a performance where you don't have that kind of thing going for you, then you sometimes have to manipulate your cameras more; you have to cut more. The biggest problem that most of us directors have is in knowing when *not* to overcut. The great tendency when you are in the booth—and all of us have it, some less than others—is that when you are on a shot for six seconds, you say, "Okay, I've seen that. I've got to change it." Everybody around you is all geared up to change, the cameramen are ready to zoom and to dolly, the T.D. is waiting for your signal and you feel like you have to make the move. You've got to say to yourself,

"Wait a minute. This is working great just where it is, on the close-up. Let's stay on this shot."

What about pretty pictures? I asked Don if there are any aesthetic principles that he applies to his work. (What came to mind as I asked this question was the old *Perry Como Show* on NBC, which was directed by Dwight Hemion, the director that Don Mischer had expressed such admiration for. There was always a single rose on a darkened stage with Como when he sang one or two of his very sentimental songs. It was a designed shot, of course—by Gary Smith, now Hemion's partner, but for many years his scenic designer—but it always worked for me. I was always touched as Como sang, and Hemion would move in on that perfectly lit, soft-focus rose. Not the quintessential example of aestheticism on television, but a lovely moment. I told Don about my enthusiasm for the shot and asked him if he looked for those kinds of moments in his shows.)

I think most directors do. You are constantly searching for that kind of thing. Now, that kind of "set" beauty is harder to do when you're doing event-oriented television, the kind of variety television that seems to be working so well today. On any special that you do there are many wonderful opportunities to do beautiful shots, and as a director, I love them, but it's primarily a matter of seeing them and taking advantage of them.

Beauty is very important, yet it is certainly not the *most* important thing. The most important thing to me is whether people find what you do interesting and entertaining. To the extent that beauty contributes to that— great.

Paul Bogart (Courtesy of the Academy of Motion Picture Arts
and Sciences.)

6

Paul Bogart: Directing
Archie Bunker

As I was sitting with Paul Bogart in his office in the back lot of the Burbank Studios in Hollywood, a huge film and television production complex that was once Warner Brothers and that now houses everything from sitcoms to feature films, all I could think of was the first time we had ever met, when he directed a production of Graham Greene's *The Potting Shed* for *The Play of the Week*—I think the year was 1962. I was fresh from the experience of producing five years of religious programs for a Sunday morning show called *Look Up and Live* on CBS, and my head was filled with the religious symbolism that I often used when my scripts didn't meet the needs of my productions.

I remembered that we were discussing the set for the play, and I was telling him some notion that I had about three telephone poles that were to be posted deep in back of the shed, which I thought might symbolize the three crosses of Calvary, giving deep religious overtones to the play—though I'm not sure Graham Greene ever intended that. Once he had heard me out, Paul started to laugh; in fact, he broke up completely—something he does quite often, a deep, resounding roar coming from his diaphragm. He has a wonderful laugh. When he stopped, he said nothing more, except to agree that some telephone poles might look fine in back of the potting shed. I must admit I was chagrined to say the least, but satisfied that I had gotten my poles. There was no more to be said, and the show went on to become one of our more modest hits on *The Play of the Week*.

Now, almost a quarter century later, hearing Paul chuckle and laugh as he told me about his work, I realized that with that unique

sense of humor, he has been able to peel away almost all the per-
siflage from the shows he has directed. It was to be an underlying
theme in our interview: his refreshing way of looking at things.

I remember the first show that I ever directed in television, which was
Carlton E. Morris' *One Man's Family* (which had been a long-running
radio show). And the reason I got to direct was that I was on as assistant
director to Eddie Kahn, who was the regular director. A sweet fella named
Dick Clemmer was the producer. And they came to me shortly after I
came on the show and said that Eddie was going to take a vacation every
four or five weeks, and I was going to direct the show when he was gone.
Anyway, when I heard that, I was terrified. I said, "I don't know how to
do that." And they said, "Please, don't bother us. We have a lot of other
problems."

And that's the way it was in 1951, 1952—producers just couldn't be
bothered—so I went into rehearsal, even though I was scared to death,
terrified at first of the traffic of the cameras. I didn't know which end of
the camera you shot out of. But once I got past that, once I made all my
mistakes and realized that there were certain rules and regulations, certain
laws of cinema and geography, and if you observed them diligently, or
broke them when you had to, you could shoot anything. Most of all, I
suddenly realized that cameras aren't what the job is; the job is people,
feelings and behavior. When I discovered that, a great big light went on
over my head.

I remember the very first note session I ever had on *One Man's Family*.
Bert Lytell, one of the grand old men of the theatre, was playing the father,
and the kids were Eva Marie Saint and Tony Randall, and I was so scared
of those actors, of what I was doing, so unconfident of my own feelings
that I didn't dare criticize their performance, even though they were sitting
around in a circle waiting for notes, and I had to say something. Bert Lytell
had just upset me with the way that he had played a scene. I didn't know
what was wrong with it; I just knew that it wasn't right. So I said to him,
"Mr. Lytell, don't you think in that scene with your grandson, you should
be more embarrassed than angry?" And he looked at me over the top of
his glasses, and he said, "No!" And that was that, right?

Well, I got cold, and my knees turned to rubber. The rest of the actors
were sitting around watching me make a fool of myself, until Eva Marie
came to my rescue, and said, "Paul, don't you think that blah, blah, blah
. . . ," and she got me off the hook by inventing something. I don't allow
that to happen anymore.

The "big light" that went on over Paul's head has obviously stayed
on through hundreds of shows, as eclectic a collection of programs
as anyone could conceive. I asked him how it all started.

I was enormously lucky. My wife and I had been puppeteers when we were young, and then I went off to war. When I came back, the puppet business went to pieces. We did it for a while, were booked for a week of performances at the old Mecca Temple by a wonderful man named Hal Friedman, who, with his partner Dave Yellen, were about to become Broadway producers, and they did our show. Dissolve—it's now 1950, and I'm driving a truck to earn enough money to feed my family, and Hal calls me up, says that he now has a show in television, and would I like to work for him? He put me on as a floor manager, and I nearly died of gratitude. I'd never earned so much money in my entire life—eighty-five dollars a week.

So I started to work in the RCA Building in New York, where NBC had its headquarters, on a show called *Broadway Open House*, which was on the air every night from eleven to twelve. And it was like a whole world opened for me. Anyway, I did that show for a while, and NBC moved me, gave me additional shows as a floor manager. I did *Your Show of Shows* with Sid Caesar and Imogene Coca for quite a while, and I did *The Aldrich Family*. God knows, I did everything they had. Eventually, I got onto *One Man's Family*, where they made me a director. I think they were pulling people out of the elevators in those days, saying "You're a director." Best of all, working as I did, I learned while I earned.

I asked him what some of the things were that he learned at that time. Was it easy for him to make the switch? Was it difficult? Did he catch on quickly?

It took me about four or five shows before I had any idea of what I was supposed to do. Then I learned first of all not to be afraid of the machinery, that the equipment was there to serve you. And that all I had to know about it was what it was capable of and what its limitations were. And there were lots of limitations then: there were turret lenses, no zooms, the cameras were big and unwieldy, the lights were hot and time was at a premium.

But you learned to work within very strict time limits, so much so that I'm still aware of time limitations, even though I don't have to work inside them anymore, doing more film than television as I am. But after I got through all that—how to shoot a show, how to look at it, how to see it best—then I addressed myself to the sense of it. It was a little bit ass-backwards, but it was then that I learned to deal with the essence of the play, the people in the play. I learned how to deal with the actors. It seems complex when you begin, and you learn slowly, but once you glimpse the truth and the path opens up for you, the way in which you treat a moment-by-moment studio situation becomes instinctive.

Did he have a visual image of what he was about to do when he
started a show, I wondered. Say he has a new script on his desk,
and he picks it up for the first time and starts to read it. Does he
see it in terms of images?

Sometimes, not always. First of all, I read it just to make some sense
out of it. I read it to see if it will make me laugh or cry. If it's a well-
written script, with good clean scenes, those scenes immediately suggest
how they should be done. Then, as you begin to move that scene inside a
set, you realize that set has to serve the scene. So certain images do present
themselves; they have to. You need a door here, you need a table there,
and the actors have to be over there somewhere. So right away you are
thinking in those terms, setting the scene. But most of all, in television,
you always work to and from the camera.

I think that this is one of the most difficult things to teach and to
learn about directing a television show. Most of us are oriented to
the proscenium arch; we watch things on a flat plane, expecting
movement left and right, as on the stage. In television, that's alien
to the nature of our lenses, which see things in a very limited arc,
depending on which end of the zoom you are using. It was best
described for me as "shooting into the short end of a funnel." Once
you can convey this to students and other aspiring directors, they
take giant steps toward developing a viable shooting style. Paul
continued,

It's what I call the Orson Welles school of shooting. He's the grandaddy
of all that shooting that we used to copy on dramatic shows, where you
try to sustain shots as long as possible because it was the wise thing to do.
You could do that, as long as you could continue to stage for the camera,
back and forth, picking up the people that you needed when you wanted
them. It was an economical way to work, not settling for lots of cuts as
directors do nowadays. It made for some interesting shows.

I wanted to include Paul in this collection of interviews because
I had always thought that he was one of the few directors in television
who could do serious drama with style and great sense, and then
instantly go to a piece of high comedy and do that with great style,
making splendid pictures along the way, in whatever milieu he was
functioning. As the conversation proceeded, I began to get some
inkling of how he managed this: it was his intense concentration on
content. I asked him about this.

It's true, that's what's important to me, where pictures aid and support content, and if they don't, they don't belong there. There's no reason to shoot pictures which don't help the story, the people, the play. I'm there to deliver the sense of a play, and if I screw that up, I'm not doing my job. I don't care if anyone knows that I've been on the set; I don't particularly want to be seen, I don't feel it necessary to leave a flourish of any kind that's peculiarly mine—a signature of some kind. But I am devoted to the text, to content. And, strangely enough, I found that as I got more involved in content, I became less and less fearful of the mechanics of the medium.

I've discussed this before in this collection: how sharply the lines were drawn in the early days of television between the technical side of the medium and the production side. Most directors in those early days came out of the theatre and were surprisingly uninvolved with the technical aspects of their job. Now almost everyone who comes into the business has been trained at some film or TV school. I've always felt that some dramatic training would be to their advantage: the more you knew, the more skilled you would become at your job. But it doesn't always work that way. I see too many young directors who are skilled at getting the job done, but the screen remains blank, devoid of ideas. Hopefully, they will read what Paul has to say about content.

But now, I was anxious to switch gears and ask him about his decision to do Archie Bunker. I told him that I had followed his career with a great deal of pleasure over the years but had to admit that I was shocked and surprised when I read that he was going to direct *All in the Family*. What an extraordinary changeover this must have been for him. I asked him about the things that went through his mind as he made the switch.

Yeah, I thought a lot about it, not because I look down on the show itself. I just didn't know whether I'd be good for it; I didn't know whether I fit in there. Carroll O'Connor's an old friend of mine. I used him a lot in the early days of television playing Irish priests, doctors, someone's uncle—he's a wonderful actor and, even more, a wonderful man to be around. They'd been asking me to do the show, and I kept saying, "But this is not for me, you know. I don't think I really know how to do this."

But then, I got caught in a money crunch, and I began to think about it very seriously, and I decided that there would be no more hospitable climate in which to work, for not only was Carroll very receptive, but Norman Lear was very warm, very anxious to have me. The show had already been on for five years, but I thought I'd take a flyer at it, see if I could apply everything I knew to this kind of work.

I said to myself, "It is, after all, a play, and these are legitimate actors, very funny, very gifted and very attuned to television." Well, how could I go wrong?

Needless to say, it was a wonderful experience. The cast of *All in the Family* were the best television actors that I ever worked with, with great theatrical instincts. They subliminally saw their camera lights going on— that sort of thing.

I have never been exposed to such a company with such concentration and such teamwork. They'd been together for a long time; the characters were set; I only had to keep them true and revitalize them.

Best of all, I was working in front of a live audience again; I hadn't been in front of a live audience for many years. And I thought, "This is the way it should be. You can learn something from an audience, and from a company like this."

So I went to work, and I said to myself, "I'll do this the way that I used to do *CBS Playhouse*, only it's funny." You see, the rules are exactly the same—you don't do anything that's out of context. I also said to myself, "If I find out in short order that the gag is supreme and that they would rather do a joke because it's a good joke, and not because it belongs, then we'll come to a parting of the ways." But I found out that wasn't the case at all. Jokes were always integral to the story line.

And they were so unselfish about their jokes. They would never keep a joke that didn't belong to them; they passed their jokes around to one another. Carroll would say to Jean Stapleton, "This is something you should be doing. It's funnier out of your mouth than it is out of mine." And they had a lot to say about their characters because by that time, after five years of doing those people, they owned these characters.

So about the best thing that I could do when I got there was to loosen everything up. I suddenly found that they were eager to have somebody bring them stuff. They were drying up, and they wanted somebody who would say, "This is working. Loosen up here. This could be a little tighter." I just shifted everything. It was a great job.

It must have been a difficult time for Paul, but I'm sure his sense of humor and his great credibility stood him in good stead as he made the transition. I wanted to hear more, so I asked him to be specific about the kind of "stuff" he brought to the show.

Stuff. For one thing, they touched one another more. I mean, there was a lot of groping around when I started on the show: Archie chased Edith up the stairs a couple of times. There was lots of physical humor—Archie would pull Edith down on his lap, for example. Sally Struthers would touch Carroll like my daughters used to touch me. There was a lot of physical intimacy that I don't recall before me.

We also spent a lot of time digging for what was really rich in the characters, and going for it. We never hesitated to go for something that wasn't funny, either—something that might stop you dead in your tracks—because we knew that we could make the switch any time we wanted, making you cry first and then making you laugh.

I had a wonderful time on that show; I learned so much from those people, about comedy timing, about the generosity of a troupe which is giving all the time, and getting back in turn, making the circle perfect. It was a great experience for me. I learned that you don't do a sitcom any differently than you would do a serious play—you just do it faster.

Next, I asked Paul if he would tell me the weekly routine of the show, describing in detail how the show functioned throughout their season, each week they were in production.

We would get together on Monday morning and read the script that was to be done in two weeks. The whole company would sit around and discuss that, all of us, the producers, the writers, the actors, and I. The writers would then take that script away, presumably to rework it, and then we would read the current week's script, which we had read on the preceding Monday and which had by now gone through that process of change.

The show wouldn't get on its feet until Tuesday, but we would still continue refashioning the whole thing right there in the studio, improvising huge chunks, throwing out what was bad, using what was good, constantly making judgements about the material. It seems that everybody on the show was a writer, including me.

By Wednesday night, we were giving a performance for the staff, the producers, and the writers. By now, the cast knew the script; they had it all memorized, with the changes and all.

That night, after everyone had left, I would stay and block my shots. I had given them no consideration until that moment; there was no time. It wasn't a complicated blocking; all I did, instinctively, was keep the actors on the stage, make sure that I had unobstructed access to their faces. Besides, it was hard to block something when there were still so many script changes going on.

Anyway, on Thursday, we'd go into the studio, do the blocking that I had worked out the night before, have a run-through, make further changes, have more note sessions and make further changes. We never let the script alone.

On Friday we came in a little bit later. It was the first day that we got any kind of a break. We didn't have to start early in the morning—I hate getting up early—and then we would have more notes because the show had been timed the previous night. We had kept a clock on it all week, but we had a more accurate timing by then. We used to leave a good hefty spread for laughter—I mean four or five minutes. I wouldn't let them stop the show unless the audience screamed.

Finally, Friday afternoon, we would have a run-through, then more notes and more changes, then a dress rehearsal with an audience present. And after that we would break for dinner, where, as we ate, we would have one final big note session where we would try to fix everything that we felt had not worked in the dress. In some cases that meant a complete rewrite and restaging. It was an hysterical time.

The sitcom is the creature of the writer, especially a successful sitcom like *All in the Family* that is trying to sustain a long run as a prelude to a successful sale in syndication. *All in the Family* was developed by Norman Lear (a writer) from a BBC series called *Till Death Do Us Part*, a story about a racist, profane garbage man in London. It had a good run on the BBC, the work of one writer, John Speight. The British have always felt very strongly about protecting the integrity of a creative work, even a situation comedy. They feel it should be the consummate work of one person, the writer who developed it, and if he decides to put it to rest for a while, so be it. Hence, the limited numbers of a show like *Fawlty Towers*, the brilliant work of the comic genius John Cleese.

As it is told here in Bogart's interview, you begin to understand the Hollywood creative process as it relates to the sitcom. Everyone has his innings with the script; everyone writes, whether he is a writer or not, although most of the production staff are writers, and that includes the director and the actors. How else can you explain thirteen years of Archie Bunker?

But now it was time to tape the show. I assumed that they had already taped their dress.

We tape everything, dress and air. And more often than you might think the dress gets on the air, or at least a good deal of it. On one show, one of the cameramen injured himself after the dress rehearsal and went to the hospital, and we sat there with the audience waiting for him to come back, but he never did. And we said, "What the hell, we'll go with the dress," and we did. I always used to cut them together anyway—the dress and air.

This surprised me, not because it was unusual to piece together a dress rehearsal and an air show but because Paul was involved in the editing process. This was unusual because most directors, especially those who free-lance, do not exercise the right to a first cut given them by their Director's Guild contract, choosing instead to go on to shooting another show, rather than going through the laborious process of editing the one they have just finished. I asked Paul whether he was involved in the cutting of the show.

Totally. No one's ever cut anything in a show I was on without my presence in the editing room. We would finish on Friday night after we had taped two performances. Then, if it were necessary, we'd do pickups, which I hate doing. I always like to shoot—cut and switch—as close to ideal as possible. To cover myself, I had two iso-positions, and I would use those to cover my mistakes, or laughs that had gone on for too long. We used those "iso's" to fill in with reactions, close-ups, stuff like that. I'd rather do that than go through a series of endless takes. I hate all that reshooting, and I just won't do it. The actors love me for it, for it meant that they'd be out of there by ten o'clock, where they'd been used to staying until one or two in the morning.

I'm not addicted to "iso" feeds, the locking of one camera into one tape recorder, especially for student productions because, in most cases, it just allows the student to slough off his blocking, feeling that he can always cover his scenes with his isolated camera, no matter what happens, and fix them in the editing. Well, I think that's one of the great myths of television production: that "you can fix something in the editing." I feel that if it wasn't there in the first place, it ain't fixable. A professional like Paul is something else again; he is always in control, no matter what he does. I asked him if he kept one of his isolated cameras on Archie (Carroll O'Connor).

Yes and no. It depends on the scene and where I think we need the coverage. I always try to be sensible about it. I don't want too much material to work with afterwards. I want to be somewhat limited, so that there aren't too many choices. I think that's important, to stay lean, to stay economical, not to give yourself too much to play with, or else it goes on forever.

Anyway, Saturday and Sunday we'd be off, and early Monday morning I'd come in and screen a 3/4-inch copy of what we'd done on Friday, go through that with the editor and construct the show from the beginning to the end, using my notes and the burn-in numbers on the 3/4 inch.

Then I would go to rehearsal and start all over again with the next week's show. That night I would go back to the editing room and see the rough cut, make a few adjustments, a few cuts for time, and that would be it. We would make our final show copy on two inch or one inch, whatever we were into at the time.

I asked Paul if he thought that was unusual, supervising the editing that way.

It is, to a degree, especially when you are talking about videotape. With film, there's all that film to play with, and everybody knows how to edit, how to put a film together. Just ask any producer, and film editor, and their assistants—it's everybody's playground.

Well, screw it; in television they can't do that. For one thing, tape is too perishable. You can't see anything on it when you pick it up; it's mylar. You can't see through it, there's nothing there and that frustrates a lot of people; it becomes a blind item for them. So it's not as easy to fool around with tape as it is with film, and consequently there aren't that many practitioners around.

I've had so many years working with tape, and in live television before that, it's become second nature to me. I know what you can do and what you can't do, and I know how to do it fast—mainly because I don't like sitting in those cold, dark editing rooms for too long. It's nice getting your show assembled and getting out in the sunshine.

And that was our routine. We took every third week off, and for a while every fourth week off. Sometimes around holidays we would get two weeks in a row off. We would do twenty-four shows a year, and that was our season.

I don't know why I asked Paul Bogart the next question, because I already knew the answer, but people's perceptions of themselves are often different than their reality. But I asked it anyway: "Are you funny, Paul?"

I think I have a wonderful sense of humor, but even better, I'm the best audience in the world. The cast of *Family* used to have me on the floor. Those people would make me laugh so much that I would get hysterical, and they loved it. I think there was a transition in their minds between me and the audience, feeling that if they could make me laugh, they could also make the audience laugh. I would just die right on the spot; they would do things that were so wonderful.

There was one night when we were taping a show in which Carroll did a take that the audience just loved, and they screamed. In the scene, Carroll walks into a bar and suddenly hears Edith's voice, singing at the piano, when he thought he had left her at home. The audience all knew how he felt about her singing, so when he stopped dead at the sound of her voice, he reacted, and then they reacted. Well, as the laughter grew, I started to laugh as I was sitting at the console, so much so that I began to hyperventilate. The whole control room began to spin, passing me by like it was a railroad train. I had to hold on to the console because I thought I was going to fall down. My script was in front of me, but I couldn't read it because it was going this way and that. Well, I finally caught it, but I couldn't find my place. I didn't know what my next camera direction was to be. And I thought to myself, "If he only keeps this up for a while longer, I will eventually collect myself," which is what happened. As the laughter grew, Carroll did a double take, and then maybe a triple take for all I knew, and they continued to laugh. As for me, eventually the room stopped swimming; I settled down, found my place and went on with the show.

But I loved every minute of it. I loved the humor, and I loved the cast. I also loved the way they made me cry. I'm a good audience.

Comedy seems to me to be the hardest thing in the world to do, on stage as well as on the screen. Our most unsuccessful broadcasts of *Play of the Week* were the comedies that we did. We did our shows in the studio without an audience, and we soon discovered that with comedy, that's like cooking dinner without the use of salt, pepper or spices. Most good comedy writers for the theatre write beats into their plays, which are the moments when the audience is expected to laugh, and the same is true in television. It makes for problems when the material isn't funny, and sitcoms increasingly turn to bad laugh tracks to fill those beats. I asked Paul how he felt about canned laughter, and if his soundtrack on *Family* was ever augmented in any way.

When we were live like that, and we edited back and forth between dress and air as we did, the track had to be augmented because the laughs wouldn't match on the crossovers, and that had to be fixed. On rare occasions, I would help a laugh that I thought I had not made clear enough to the audience, but which deserved it. But there was a minimum of tinkering with the track; the laughs were big enough as they were.

After we dropped the audience in the last year of the show, it was all laugh-tracked, and that was no fun at all. I just didn't like that.

Paul is a television gypsy if ever I met one. He keeps shuttling back and forth between New York and Hollywood, working for the commercial end of the business one week and public broadcasting the next. He's in a serious drama mode one week and in a sitcom mode the next. I asked him if this didn't make him a little schizophrenic, making the transition back and forth between coasts and dramatic styles.

Not in the slightest. It confuses everybody else; it keeps them wondering where I belong. I think that's one of the joys of doing the kind of work I do—that I can move around, do straight drama, and then do funny things if I feel like it. It gives one a chance to stretch and not be stuck in one place.

Over lunch with Paul, prior to our interview, he was very negative about something he had done on *American Playhouse*,* and I pushed this point. I wanted to know if he had different standards for commercial and noncommercial drama but even more, from a purely personal point-of-view, if he had difficulty shifting gears from a Hollywood frame of mind—if when he came back east and saw a serious piece of drama, did he say, "God, that's a pretentious piece of crap"?

That's a danger I'm aware of, but in the case of the particular play we are talking about, which I'd rather not mention, incidentally, I truly felt that the text was slight, somewhat pretentious, literary, nondramatic. It just didn't have the proper shape of a play.

Now I had learned many years before that when you don't trust the material, you tend to overproduce it. It's a cynical thing to say, I know, but it works. Therefore, when material is tottering, you shore it up with as much ambience as you can. You don't linger too much on the material because it's not strong enough. So what you do is you build a whole life around the material. For example, make sure that you have a very versatile set, so that you can get interesting pictures. A rainstorm doesn't hurt, either. . . . Now, as I said, I'm being cynical, but the fact is that those ambient possibilities help to fill in the missing life of the play. If the thing you are covering is working well, there's no need to jazz up the picture. There's not even a reason to cut if the actor or performer is doing the material the right way. You can only hurt their performance by trying to juice things up, trying to dazzle your audience with your cutting and your shooting, when all you are doing is distracting them.

I want the audience to pay attention. I've learned that lesson a hundred different times in my life. I try and climb into the woodwork at times and let the artist carry the ball all by himself. I did *Ages of Man*, with Sir John Gielgud, which we did on film, incidentally, and I forgot my own good advice. I tried not to interfere with his performance, but I couldn't keep my hands off of it. I had underestimated the power of this great artist, and as a result, I overproduced it. I simply did too much. I didn't need all those lighting effects, all that movement.

I said to him at one point, "Sir John, when you're doing, 'How sweet the moonlight sleeps upon this bank,' I thought I might bring in a little

*A dramatic series produced every winter on PBS.

reflected ripple in the water," and he answered me in the flattest voice possible, "That would be *lovely*."

When I did *Mark Twain Tonight*, with Hal Holbrook, I think I had my act together a little better. Now this was just as thrilling to me as working with Gielgud. It's just great to be locked up with these people in a rehearsal hall for three or four weeks, just working on something. They're doing their number just for you. When we finally got to the shooting, I had a lot of pictures of Hal walking across the stage, sitting down, standing up, and that was only the first run-through.

And then I said to myself, "I'm doing too much again. Let's take all this *chasarai** out of here; we don't need this." The second run-through was much straighter, less distracting from the performer and his art, and that's the way you should do it. As I said, you just have to crawl into the woodwork and let the performer shine. You can't get caught between him and the audience.

Paul's eclecticism as a director was something I wanted to explore. As much as anyone I know, Paul goes back and forth between film and videotape, between single camera and multiple camera, between working for the big screen and the small one. I asked him first about videotape versus film.

Different worlds. Videotape is, for me, best for sustained performance, and for what I call dense material—ideas and dialogue which are the essence of theatre. That's what you're selling on videotape. Even if it's a comedy show, you're dealing with ideas—comic ideas, maybe—but still ideas.

Film requires air, space, time, all of which you don't have in a television studio. So the studio becomes the place for clever ideas and good talk. You're not working with space; your sets are limited in size. But if you're on film, that's something else again; you have the world to play with. And even if you are dealing with small ideas and spare dialogue in your film, action begins to take over, size takes over; you're impelled into bigger movement, and all that. It's a whole different world.

How did he feel about working with a single camera, as opposed to multiple cameras?

I'm comfortable either way. Most of the time that's a producer's decision based on what they feel is suitable. You light better in one angle than you do in multiple angles—everybody knows that. I've even used two film cameras to give me added coverage when I need it—in a scene that's going to move very quickly, for example.

*A Yiddish word which means, in this context, things that are extraneous.

In a studio, working with videotape, I think multiple cameras are preferable, but I like working with single cameras just fine.

As I did with everyone else that I interviewed, I wanted to know if there were any aesthetic principles that he applied to his work. Did he ever set out from the start just to make pretty pictures?

I always try and make pretty pictures, but I try not to choose the pretty picture over the necessary one. I do like a well-composed picture, a well-balanced picture and a well-lit picture. I like the camera to be low, simply because I don't like to shoot down at the top of your head. I want to see your eyes; I like to be down here when you're sitting, I want to be sitting with you. When you rise, I want to get up as you do.

The height of the lens is terribly important to me. I don't like people who operate their cameras at a height which is convenient for them, which happens a lot in television. In the live days, I used to block all the high shots with the tall cameramen, and all the low shots with the short ones, and that's the truth. Because I knew that was where they would be when we got on the air.

I like my shots to be visually arresting, when they should be, when they can help the play. When it looks good to have a deep shot with lots of shadows, I want it; when it looks good to be looking at a blank wall because there's something dry and flat about what's going on at that moment, that's the way I want it.

My memory of Paul, in the few times that we had worked together, or that I had seen him work, was that he was one of the most amiable men around. He laughed when I told him this and cynically remarked that he was "one of the nicest people in the world." I asked him what he did when he found that he had to push people around—cameramen, for example.

I don't push them; I just tell them to do it. I say, "No, no, no, no, no, this is the way we have to do this." In the studio, on location, I'm the last word. Not that I close myself off to suggestions. A lot of cameramen come to me and say, "Wouldn't it be great if . . . " or "Could I do . . . " and I say, "Yeah, please, be my guest. Why didn't you think of this yesterday?" I love that—I love it when the cameramen come in with ideas.

And I usually give them their shots. I don't care who makes the show better. If anyone can contribute, that's great with me. My name's going to go on the show anyway. If someone thinks that they can make a show any better, and I think it's going to work, too—well, then, I'm happy.

I asked him if he was selective in picking his cameramen. Did he find that one camera person was different from another? Did he try to work with people that he had worked with before?

The answer to all of those questions is sometimes. Sure, some cameramen are better than others. If you are going to do a show for one of the networks, you try and search out the best cameramen they have. You may have worked with them before; they may have come highly recommended. But I'll take a chance on any of them, even the new ones. I do it all the time, and I'm rarely sorry.

When I did *The Shady Hill Kidnapping* for public broadcasting, we made it in Connecticut with the PBS station there, and they had never done a dramatic show before. They had done some local stuff, some PBS feeds, that kind of thing, and they were just terrified at the idea of doing a full-scale drama and, at the same time, thrilled at the prospect.

And on the first day there, they had arranged a meeting with the whole crew, primarily to get acquainted. When I arrived, and looked around, there were little pastries, and coffee, and soft drinks, and a sea of faces, all sitting around, looking at me with fear in their eyes, asking "Just what the hell have we gotten into here?"

Somebody from the station said to me, "They're scared," and it just broke my heart, so I said to them, "Listen, I know that you ordinarily don't do this, and I know it's going to be a heavy job for you, and I hope that you feel you've got the talent for this. But if you don't, what matters more to me is that you're nice. If you're all nice people, we're going to get through all this beautifully. If you're talented as well, we're going to get through this magnificently. But I don't want you here if you're talented and a son-of-a-bitch. If that's the case, leave now. I just don't want anybody here who isn't nice."

And they all smiled and were so pleased with what I had said that we all became the greatest of friends. Needless to say, they were as nice and as talented as people can be, and it was a beautiful show, and those people from Connecticut did beautiful work on it, indistinguishable from most of the work that is done on the networks, really.

It was now about three o'clock and Paul said that he had to go back to work. He was shooting one of the George Burns *Oh, God!* movies at the Burbank lot, and, as always, he was quite upbeat about what he was doing. That was his style, and something we all should learn to do.

As a final question, I asked him if there were still things that he wanted to do.

Yeah, I'd still like to make some more good movies. I'd like to make some more good television shows—the only place left for them now is public television. I love working there. They're after whole different things; it's always been like that. They want to do something that you can't see anywhere else, and that pleases me.

7

Lloyd Tweedy: Directing Corporate Communications

Lloyd Tweedy is an anachronism in the control room: he's the only director that I know who comes to work in a three-piece suit. Occasionally, in the heat of the studio and his directing chores, he will carefully remove his jacket and vest and hang them on a hanger behind his chair at the console, but his tie still remains carefully tied, and you know that his white shirt never suffers from "ring around the collar."

I have known Lloyd for a long time. In fact, at one time our careers paralleled, he working for the Sunday morning religious program *Directions* at ABC, while I was doing the same at CBS, producing and directing *Look Up and Live*. Over the years, I guess we have formed a kind of mutual admiration society, the two of us. If I was producing something that I couldn't direct myself, or if I needed a second director on one of my telethons, I always called upon Lloyd, knowing that I would always get an intelligent piece of work from him that never had to be supervised. Conversely, when he started hiring free-lance directors at IBM, he called on me.

One chilly morning last fall, I talked with Lloyd in his office, which is located in one of the largest of International Business Machines' many facilities, planted deep in the heart of Westchester County, about thirty-five miles north of New York City. I knew this building very well because until about five years ago, it had housed two complete television studios, and I had gone in and out of this fine facility many times, contracted to do any number of diverse directorial tasks for IBM. This was my introduction to corporate communications, which has become an important tool for the Amer-

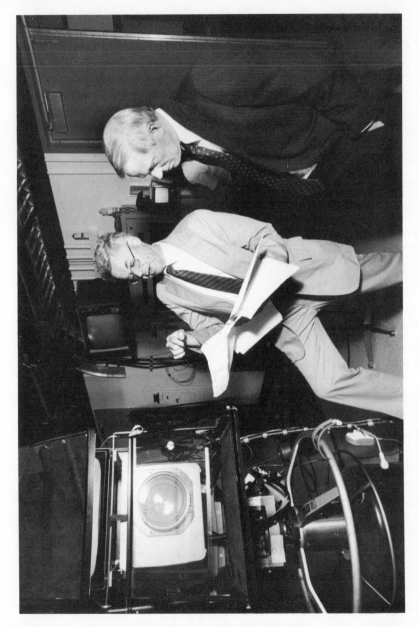

Lloyd Tweedy (left) with unidentified actor.

ican way of doing business. I asked Lloyd Tweedy how it all began at IBM.

IBM began experimenting with videotape and videotape playback in 1970, as it was being developed. David Shefrin, whom you know, had just been hired from ABC News to examine the use of television for possible internal and external communications use. Anyway, Dave knew the president of the SONY Corporation—I don't know how he got to know him, but he did—and SONY was most interested in cooperating with IBM, testing some of their new equipment. So they were very willing to provide IBM with some of the first 3/4-inch U-Matic machines.

Early in 1972, IBM bought the first three hundred of those machines, and they were in the business of videotaping and playback for internal communications. We built the studios here in Westchester, and we were in business.

Decisions are never made thoughtlessly in a corporation like IBM, and to understand some of the reasoning that went into this decision, I felt that there had to be some understanding of the size of the company itself and how difficult it must have been before television for IBM to stay in touch with all its employees. I asked Lloyd to give me some figures.

At the end of 1987, IBM had about 228,000 domestic employees and about 390,000 worldwide. Now, domestically, these employees are spread over 650 branches. As far as the rest of the world is concerned, I can't even begin to tell you. Each overseas IBM operation is, in effect, just that—an overseas operation, where perhaps one percent of the employees are Americans or other nationals, and all the rest are natives of the country where the branch is located.

The first year we moved into the studio here at 1133, we taped perhaps thirty programs. At the peak of our output, in the late 1970s, we did over one hundred. They ran the gamut from sales pitches and new product reports to corporate messages by the chairman. But I think our enthusiasm overcame our objectivity, and we probably did too many videotapes and overloaded the branches with shows. There was just too much stuff coming in, and they didn't have time to look at it all. So we cut back on production. By 1986, when the studio was shut down temporarily for a major building renovation (which is still going on), the number of videotapes projected for the coming year did not justify reopening it. So the technical staff was reassigned to other areas, remaining tape production was supervised by staff producers using outside vendors and the studio was permanently shut down.

At present, IBM continues its commitment to videotape, and production and distribution go on, but at a more useful pace.

I asked Lloyd to give me a couple examples of the kind of things they produced in the studios in Westchester, the kind of things they "overloaded the branches with."

Most of it was what we describe as "marketing support" material—how to use existing IBM systems, new applications of those systems. There was also a lot of what we call executive videotapes, where division presidents or other top executives give progress reports on how well their particular division is doing in meeting their goals.

I know it sounds pretty dull to someone not involved with the company, but we also had our moments, just as you do in any studio. I remember one time we did a very involved marketing support show, using five very busy executives, and we had the luxury of their presence for two days: one for rehearsal, one for taping, and that took some doing, believe me. By the way, we did most of our shows like live shows, switching them in the control room.

On this particular show, we had a very involved set, with some complicated furniture placement. We planned it so that when we cut from scene to scene, we would replace the furniture in the upcoming scene while we were taping the current scene. It was all very carefully rehearsed; we had marks on the floor for everything. It took a twelve-hour day to set it all up.

When we came back into the studio the following morning for what was to be our taping day, the cleaning people had been there overnight, waxed the linoleum to a beautiful sheen and in the process erased every one of our marks. Needless to say, we "winged" it, and it worked pretty well.

Lloyd had been hired by IBM primarily as a director, and that was his role at the beginning, but as time went by, his role and his involvement changed. The number of shows that came out of Westchester was so great that Lloyd wasn't able to direct them all. He was asked to bring in other directors, like myself, to help carry the load.

We began to use the studio for all kinds of crazy stuff. We even had Jim Henson and some of his puppeteers in on one occasion, thanks to a very talented man by the name of Dave Lazer, who was once with the Office Products Division, where he developed the use of video for them.

The Office Products Division was quite different from the rest of IBM's divisions in that their customers were at the office manager level, the secretarial level, not at the data processing director level. Consequently, they often used a totally different approach with their customers, and one of them was humor.

So Lazer came up with the idea of latching onto Jim Henson and the Muppets long before they achieved national recognition. Henson responded enthusiastically to the idea and worked very closely with Lazer in developing all kinds of crazy approaches to customers and salesmen alike. In one case, he developed a funny kind of "sell, sell, sell" module using Kermit the Frog, to exhort the salesmen to do a bigger and better job. It was highly successful, and Office Products used it over and over again. Shortly thereafter, Lazer severed his relationship with IBM and joined Henson. He's now the executive producer of all the Muppet movies.

By this time, I was no longer actively directing, and in 1982, I agreed to become a manager—my official title was Manager, Film and Television Programs—and I wound up with all the producers and directors reporting to me. I got away from actual studio operations, and I discovered that I liked that; I liked working with people, trying to bring out the best in them. Well, that lasted for five years, at which time the decision was made to shut the studio down, and there was a reorganization.

But Lloyd's job was safe, and he knew it. IBM's personnel policies are extraordinary—they never fire anybody unless it's for cause. And being the fine employee and citizen that he was, there was no way they were going to let Lloyd go. They changed his role, and the work continued.

Well, I am currently responsible for executive videotapes, as part of a group known as the Field Television Network. Contrary to the general pattern in broadcasting, IBM has turned to live telecasting. They developed, first on an experimental basis, and now as a very active part of their communication structure, a live satellite broadcast network that is still growing.

This network currently reaches about three hundred locations and does over a hundred broadcasts a year. It goes to what is called a "niche" audience. In other words, the people that are particularly interested in one piece of software, that can sometimes be a very small part of that branch office. That's the great plus of this limited network, that it doesn't swallow up an entire branch's time.

Like everything at IBM, it's very efficiently run. A broadcast schedule is sent out ahead of time, so people can mark their calendars for a particular broadcast that they think might be relevant and also invite customers that they think might be interested. It's part of IBM's current thrust toward partnership with their customers.

The projection is that every branch, eventually, will have one or two conference rooms in which a monitor can pick up a live satellite feed. It's one-way video, two-way audio. Anyone who wants to will be able to call an 800 number and ask the broadcaster anything he wants that is relevant to the thrust of the telecast.

I asked Lloyd if this new "niche" program had superseded all the other IBM broadcasting commitments.

No, it has augmented them. There is a corporate education center in Thornwood called C Net, just up the road here a bit, that's deeply immersed in television, and it's a brand new complex. It was completed about three years ago and offers a high-level technical education.

Another is a program called the IBM Satellite Educational Network— ISEN. That's fed to about twenty different cities in the United States, and it's primarily for IBM customers. I believe they even pay to go there.

Strangely, it's not as structured as you might think. Each one of these programs operates independently. The Field Television Network that I am a part of and ISEN have very little to do with each other, just as the Field Television Network and C Net have very little to do with each other. We're all pretty independent in the way we do things. I doubt if there is any redundancy because we are all aiming at different audiences.

Now I wanted to return to Lloyd's personal involvement as a director. I explained that my primary interest in these interviews had been the aesthetic choices that directors make. In Lloyd's case, because most of the work he had done had been for internal company use only, and it never saw the light of any station broadcast day, I wondered if the programs that were done at IBM suffered aesthetically because of that limited exposure.

No, I don't think so. IBM is known for quality, and they always attempt to achieve it. It's a mandatory element in every product that they put out, and that permeates everything that they do, so if a TV program is going to be produced by an IBM facility, you know damn well it's going to be a first-rate program.

Then, too, IBM is quite marvelous about deferring to quality people who they think know about the things that IBMers might be lacking in, looking for guidance and development through them. We're continually bringing in outside suppliers and contractors, even in television.

There's a long tradition at IBM of a strong commitment to the visual arts; that even predates my coming to the company. For example, IBM's involvement with Charles and Rae Eames. I'm sure that you know of their work; they were architects, designers, visual artists par excellence: the

Eames chair; the kind of thing they did for IBM at the New York World's Fair; the films and exhibits they did for IBM. And this was true of a number of other top designers and film makers. A high standard was set throughout the company, and it's still true. The Eames influence is everywhere, from brochure designs to office furniture, and this, of course, influences our personal work as employees. You feel that you've got to keep up those standards.

I asked Lloyd if he could be more specific and tell me some of the things that he did to ensure this kind of quality.

There were a great many! But what comes to mind when you ask me that has nothing to do with design. I've always felt that my most difficult task here at IBM was to bring out the best in the executives that we made into performers for our shows. As you can guess, they were all nonprofessionals that we tried to give a professional look to. Interestingly enough, most of them had a marketing background, were very knowledgeable in their field and were used to making presentations and pitches. All I tried to do was to help them get rid of any concern or fear that they might have had in using the medium and convince them that television was just another tool that they could use profitably and enjoy.

Not that we told them too much. It's really almost more the things that you don't tell them. You don't tell them how to read a line, for example, but you do tell them about the intimate nature of television and how the camera comes to them, so there's no need to make a speech. We tell them not to use their hands too much, not to gesture excessively, that sort of thing. Most of all, we try to put them at ease and try not to limit their natural enthusiasm. You let them do their own thing; most of them are used to being before the public anyway, and they do it pretty well.

In those glory years at IBM, when the studio was operating at full force, Lloyd Tweedy was more producer than director, controlling most of the studio's support elements. There were times I felt that he operated like a one-man community theatre, controlling scenic design, the building of sets, costumes, etc. (Because IBM executives were normally addicted to white shirts and blue suits as their normal mode of dress, Lloyd even arranged for a stock of off-white shirts in all sizes to be readily available for studio use by IBMers not conversant with high contrast.) I asked him about this side of his work.

Things just don't happen in television; someone has to make them happen, and I was always out in the studio assisting in whatever we did, but

I had a lot of great help. We used to have two designers on staff who had done everything from design brochures to stage business shows, and they became our set designers. Mark Pike, whom you know, was one, and he could do anything. And then, I did bring George Corrin from ABC in on a couple of occasions. But for the most part, our own designers were able to make the transition between business shows and video fairly easily, and we had some wonderful sets as a result of that collaboration. Arthur Clark used to be in charge of all that—Clark is an outstanding, most talented designer. He is now exhibit designer of the IBM Gallery, which is at 590 Madison Avenue in New York City.

We could do almost anything and everything out of that studio. We even went on remotes. I can remember our first big video conference; this was about five or six years ago—long before the Field Television Network had been set up. We took over the ballroom of the Tarrytown Hilton, here in Westchester, and completely rebuilt it. I called in George Corrin to design the set, and he built a sort of amphitheatre.

I had a camera on a huge crane inside the ballroom and three other additional cameras. We used Reeves Television as our supplier, and we worked out of their remote truck which was parked outside the hotel. The shoot took three days, and the eventual air show was three hours long. There was tremendous logistical involvement, and everyone knocked themselves out.

I think the most difficult thing about this kind of a show is that you don't get much time with your talent, the executives who do the show. So you've got to rehearse everything but your talent ahead of time, so that everybody knows what their job is, and when executives come in, it's a piece of cake for them; they can easily fit into the comfortable environment that you've set for them. I don't mean to keep harping on this, but you just can't make too many demands on these top guys. They're very good about things like camera switching if you put arrows on the teleprompter showing them which way they have to go—they can swing with that. But you can't ask them to do a lot of movement, difficult staging, choreography, things of that nature. You just have to make it as easy as possible for them, so that you use their time to optimum value. If you don't do that, and they feel that you are wasting their time, you'll lose them.

As I mentioned in my introduction to this piece, I had always felt that Lloyd was a bit of a paradox in television—he was someone who would have been much more at home in the board room of a major corporation. I guess his position in the offices and studios of one of the nation's largest corporations should not have been that much of a surprise, and when I began to question him about some of his early family and job history, I discovered that my instincts were correct:

How did I get into this business? My father was an investment broker, and I guess I sort of went astray. One of the things that influenced me was that I had an uncle of whom I was very fond, my mother's brother, and he was very debonair, a bon vivant if there ever was one. We lived in Hingham, Massachusetts, which is a suburb of Boston. Hingham was quite rural in those days. My uncle lived in Manhattan, at the Yale Club, and was one of the top people at *Promenade* magazine. He had an office at the top of the Chrysler Building, with one of those art deco curved windows to look out of. I can remember visiting him in his office and being in a cloud—in more ways than one. And then he'd take me to lunch at the Yale Club, and I thought, "This is the life to live, not as dull as living on twenty-eight acres in the back woods of Hingham."

Anyway, I started to participate in the dramatic groups at our high school and was cast in a one-act play that won a local contest and went on to Emerson College in Boston for a final play-off. I was playing a priest consoling a poor woman whose husband had had it during the French Revolution. Well, I was pretty heavy in those days, much heavier than I am now, and after that bit of action, I was supposed to turn around and sit in a chair a few feet upstage. As I sat, the chair went out from under me, and you can imagine the rest. The whole audience started to laugh, and we brought the curtain down—that was the end of the play.

I expressed a hope that it wasn't the end of his acting career.

Well, I went on to do one more role in my freshman year at college. This was the big time for me, Williams College, a college production, and unfortunately, I got panned royally for my performance in the college paper, so I said, "The heck with that. I'll work behind the scenes."

And then I got a job working at the college radio station as an announcer, and in the summer worked for a commercial radio station in Ware, Massachusetts. In fact, those were the call letters of the station—W–A–R–E. It was big polka country, and as a consequence, I got to know every polka that was ever written. On Saturday morning, I had a program called "Uncle Bud," where I would bring in six or seven little kids from the area and play children's records for them. It was a fun summer.

When I got back to college, I worked at the North Adams station as a part-time disc jockey, and radio got into my blood. Well, I majored in English, and when I graduated, a fraternity brother of mine told me about an aunt of his who was working for NBC in New York. She was the wife of a very well known pediatrician at the time, Dr. L. Emmett Holt, and she was working for NBC developing a medical series that was intended for the limited network that existed at that time.

Well, I called her—this was in 1949—and she had no work for me, but she did tell me about something called the Television Workshop. So I decided, "What the heck, I'll go and give this Television Workshop a try." The Holts had a townhouse on East 52nd Street where River House now stands, and they took me in; it was all very posh. And I enrolled in the Television Workshop, a three-month course, and I found it fascinating because I knew absolutely nothing about TV, and we got to do absolutely everything. At the end of the course—I think there were about 108 television stations in the country at the time, and I think that I wrote to nearly every one, sent them my résumé, and the first one that came back with an offer was in Pittsburgh, the Dumont affiliate there. So I moved out of the Holts' townhouse and took the train to Pittsburgh and started to work.

It didn't pay a helluva lot, that job in Pittsburgh, but I sure was excited by it, for there I was, doing what I wanted to do—work in television. The only problem was, as I soon discovered, that the station had no production facilities whatsoever. All it did was broadcast the Dumont feed out of New York.

So, I waited around, and about all we did in that year was one football game for the Dumont network, but I did get involved with that, had the fun of climbing a tower to help some technician put a line up, and I almost froze in the process.

Anyway, a year did pass, and facilities for production finally did begin to develop, and my boss at the time, a guy named Don Stewart, hired some Dumont alumnus from New York as his production manager, and I felt that I should have had the job. When I told this to Stewart, he said, "You're too valuable to me. I want you to stay with me, be my assistant." Well, I couldn't see it. All I was doing was visiting clients with Stewart, principally as his chief coffee getter.

So I said, "If that's the case, I've got to move on because I want to get into production." He told me to take a week off and go home to think about it, and then "come back and we'll talk." Before I left, I talked to the guy that they had hired from New York, the new production manager, Les Arries, and he told me, "Listen, on the way back, stop off in New York and talk to Eric Herud at Dumont—they're dying for people in production."

And I did. Eric was sort of the equivalent of a program director for WDTV in New York, the Dumont flagship station, and Les was right—they were desperate for bodies. The Ambassador Theatre had just been taken over by Dumont, and they were about to go on the air with a program called *Star Time*, which featured Benny Goodman's sextet, Frances Langford, Lou Parker, and the original Bickersons. The Bickersons were created for that show. In fact, the whole thing was a very clever and original show, and it turned out to be a fabulous hit for Dumont.

Anyway, Herud sent me over to the Ambassador, and before I went home, I had a job as a technician, a cable puller. I became a member of the technicians union and started making pretty good money, doing whatever I was told. I knew nothing about being an engineer, but I did work on all sorts of wonderful shows, like *Star Time*, the first *Jackie Gleason Show*, *Bishop Sheen*, *Captain Video* with Al Hodge, and all those other wonderful Dumont shows.

I commented to Lloyd that I thought it was rather strange to be hired as a technician when he had a theatrical and radio background and was, even more, a graduate from a prestigious eastern college.

They were desperate for people, and they thought I had a bent for that kind of thing. Besides, the work I was doing really didn't need a technical background. You don't need to be an engineer to be able to hold a cable behind a cameraman and keep it out of his way while he's dollying back. And when I became a mike operator, it doesn't take any special talent to hold a mike in front of the performer and keep it out of camera range. And for some strange reason, when I went on to become a cameraman, I became a pretty good cameraman.

I really enjoyed it, despite the fact that I'm a rotten still photographer. I did very well as a cameraman and besides, loved every minute of it. And even though I had told Dumont that I wanted to be on the production side of things, and Dumont kept saying, "Yeah, we'll put you over there eventually," they obviously needed me where I was. So I stayed, and by that time I was making very good money, so I didn't push the move any further. Well, this lasted until 1955, when my world suddenly went black, and Dumont folded. I was suddenly out of a job.

Lloyd's success as a cameraman seemed very relevant to me. The camera eye is the tip of the director's index finger, a direct road to his brain and his heart, and not too surprisingly, over the years, a great many cameramen have moved into control rooms as successful directors. Once again, it is not my intention to demean technicians and the things they do, but I do believe that aestheticism can sometimes be revealed through instinct rather than talent, through practice rather than pedantry, and years behind a camera can help develop those instincts—for some people. In other words, you don't have to be a bloody genius to learn the skills that are necessary, as Lloyd describes it, "to be on the production side."

I asked him how he finally did break in to the production side of things.

It took a little time; I was out of work for six months, and I became pretty desperate. I didn't want to ask my family for money, so I was living in the YMCA. And then, as it always happens, I was offered two jobs at the same time. One was with *McCall's* magazine, again through somebody I knew—as a space salesman, making eighteen thousand bucks a year, plus commission, which was a pretty good salary back in 1955.

On the same day, I was invited over to ABC and offered a job as a production assistant, right at the bottom of the production line, for sixty bucks a week. I was told that I would be working on *The Voice of Firestone*. Well, they walked me into a rehearsal, and there was Howard Barlow conducting the Firestone orchestra, and Rise Stevens was doing this great aria. What can I say? I was completely starstruck. I think I would have paid them to take the job. So I went to work at ABC.

I started off as a production assistant on *Firestone*, and from there went on to become an assistant director, and then a director. My first assignment as a director was a program called *Directions*, which used to be ABC's religious "must-do" program every Sunday morning, and that was a mar-velous opportunity for a director because everybody loved to do those shows, and we used to get the best of the New York talent to work on them for very little pay, whatever minimum union scale was.

Wiley Hance was the producer of *Directions*. Wiley's still around, in-cidentally. I see his credit on the *Mark Russell Comedy Hour*, which PBS does out of Buffalo. Anyway, those were wonderful years for me. Inter-estingly, those *Directions* sets were always put up in the big ABC studio; it was Sunday morning, and rather than let the studio go dark, they let us use it, and we just went wild with all that space, went completely overboard with our sets.

That big studio was located about halfway between the local ABC offices and the network's offices, and everyone would use it as a short cut between the two spaces. One day Dave Shefrin, who was the news director for WABC at the time, wandered through and introduced himself—he was on his way to check some news item at the network—and began questioning me about the set. I didn't realize the important part that he would even-tually play in my career, or I guess I would have paid a hell of a lot more attention to him than I did.

I was a director at ABC for about thirteen years, and then, in 1968, I felt that it was time that I went and did something else. I just knew that there were other things that I could do as a free-lancer—so onwards and upwards.

I did about two years of free-lance, most of it for PBS. ABC did call me back periodically; I was the pool director for the Apollo 13 space shot; I had done Apollo 10, 11, and 12 while I was still on staff at ABC. But, as I said, I did most of my work for public broadcasting during this period. I remember one show that I did called *Meet the Mayors*, which took place at the mayor's mansion in Detroit, during the annual National Conference of Mayors. They had a business meeting in the afternoon, then a cocktail party, and ended with a formal dinner and some speeches. As the evening wore on, tongues started to wag a little bit more loosely than they should have, and we captured it all on tape. I can tell you it made for a fascinating and fun show, but I'm not sure that PBS ever covered the Mayors Conference again.

I did this for a while, and then I got a call from my cohort at ABC, Dave Shefrin (I was on vacation with my family in Cape Cod at the time), wondering if I could come to IBM for a month as a consultant, that IBM was trying out the use of television for internal communications, and he thought I might be very helpful to them. So I said, "Sure," and one thing led to another, and the consultancy was renewed, and then renewed again and again, until before I knew it, five years had gone by, and I either had to join the company or end the relationship. I had lost most of my freelance contacts by that time, and as I thought about the move, against the advice of an awful lot of my friends, I decided to join IBM. Everyone thought that I would miss the challenge, the creativity, and the fun of working for the network, and that I would find IBM stultifying. But just the opposite turned out to be true; it was a great move for me.

I knew a great deal about IBM's entry into the field of corporate communications. I had known Dave Shefrin fairly well; he was news director at WABC, and I talked to him about the time he was quitting the station and joining IBM. Dave was a very vigorous man, very intelligent, very strong willed, very singular, and I asked Lloyd if he thought that it was the force of Dave's personality that sold television to IBM, or that there was a genuine need at the company for something that would solve their internal communications problems.

As I understand it, the company was growing so fast in the sixties that Tom Watson, Jr., who was chairman at the time, was concerned that management would get out of touch with the employees, and he wanted to see if he could find some way in which the various parts of the company could communicate with each other a little bit more readily. So Dave was hired as a television advisor to the corporate staff. I am not conversant with the details of that move, but I do know that Dave, after looking at the situation, offered several different proposals. One was to create a live network between corporate headquarters at Armonk and several other Westchester IBM locations. With his news experience he knew that he could set up a round robin situation that wouldn't be terribly expensive, and they would have the interaction that they needed.

Another plan was just to start a videotape network, creating things on videotape and distributing them throughout the company. Well, they decided on the second plan and started moving into it very cautiously. They rented a building in Greenwich, Connecticut, not too far from White Plains, and started transforming it into a television studio. Luckily, it was a barn that had already been changed into a film and still photography studio by a photographer named John Peckham. The best thing about it was that it was out of the way, and nobody knew what was going on there. It was a very rural setting. Dave told me that when he was shown the location for the first time by Peckham, he made a point of mentioning that there was a stocked pond out in back and that there were seven fishing poles in the studio, and "you are welcome to use the pond and fish any time that you're there."

Needless to say, Dave never got a chance to fish. He was too busy making it into a TV studio, and in his projections, he was looking ahead to the day when we would have a real studio, so he bought state-of-the-art Norelco cameras and all the best recording and editing equipment he could get his hands on.

Dave knew that this building we are sitting in right now, 1133 Westchester, was under construction, in the final stages of being finished. And in the basement of this building a screening room had been planned. Well, Dave must have gotten wind of this somehow and convinced IBM to turn the space into a broadcast facility with two studios, playback and editing space, a makeup room, a scenic dock—anything and everything that one might need.

So before we knew it, we were in these brand new studios in Westchester. At the beginning, there were only seven IBM locations able to play the tapes that were being made. But in due time, every location in the company had 3/4-inch U-Matic machines, and the shows taped at 1133 Westchester were being distributed around the world.

Eighteen years have now passed since Lloyd Tweedy left ABC and the free-lance scene, making the changeover to IBM and the world of corporate communications. I asked him if he had any regrets now about making the move.

No, none at all. As I said earlier, I think I feel more gratified than I would have if I were still at the networks. This has been a very satisfying move, from both a security point of view and an artistic one.

IBM has been very good in giving us all the support that we asked for, when we needed it. And they look for our professional and artistic advice on just how far they can go, and in what direction. For example, we never purchased any digital post-production equipment because it was all changing so rapidly, we felt, and we never did any advanced post-production in our editing rooms. We did a lot of editing—we had AMPEX editing, a Grass Valley switcher, 1 inch, 3/4 inch, and QUAD recording and playback, but if we needed digital enhancement, we'd go to a New York post-production house to provide that.

The studio equipment was all the best, and we tried to be very innovative in its use. As a matter of fact, I think IBM was one of the first places in the country in which the control room included a monitor with the teleprompter feed. The free-lance directors who worked for us saw its use here and took it into the networks.

If you are working for IBM, you will have nothing but the best in the way of technical advancement and development. We were always in the forefront of everything that was being done in television.

As I recall, Lloyd continued to direct about one out of three shows that were being done at IBM, and every once in a while took a short leave of absence to free-lance, primarily for ABC. I asked him if he still maintained his membership in the Director's Guild of America, if he still considered himself an active working director.

Yes, I do. When I first came to IBM in 1970, and over the next ten years or so, I would regularly take a biannual leave of absence and work either the convention or an election with ABC News. The company encouraged me to do it. For one thing, IBM liked me getting back in the field, bringing back information about the latest in technical development and procedure.

And, of course, I loved doing it. I enjoy that crazy atmosphere that sweeps the convention hall, and the last-minute panic that takes over. The last really exciting one that I did was in 1980, the Republican National Convention in Detroit. I was responsible for what they called perimeter control, and I had six RF cameras that I was in charge of. They were on station wagons, so you had to proceed to a certain drop point in order to get your signal through.

I also had two hard-line cameras around the convention hall that would spot a candidate leaving the hotel, perhaps secretively, and they would try and get a bead on them. The big question at that convention was who was going to be the vice-presidential candidate. Reagan was, of course, the presidential nominee, and everyone was playing games with who it would be. Was it going to be George Bush, or was it going to be Jerry Ford? There was a lot of last-minute excitement about following these candidates, and switching cameras from RF feed and getting them hard-lined so that they could be picked up—and, meanwhile, staying on the air with another camera that already was hard-lined. It was very exciting stuff.

One of the things that has always given me pause as a teacher of television production relates to the fact that I have introduced a number of great people to the wonders of the control room over the years, and then I feel that I desert them—I leave them out on a limb. I always feel that I should have a list of great places where they can go and work, rather than letting them fend for themselves in the job market. So I kind of jumped at Lloyd about the job opportunities in corporate communications. Were there any, and were they worth considering if there were?

The answer is, of course, there are, and, yes, they should be considered. I believe there's a much better chance today of finding a video career in corporate communications than there is in broadcasting. At the last I heard, all three networks had job freezes on. They are into an era of staying lean, taking as much profit out of the networks as possible. I suppose there are job opportunities if you go to the small stations out in the boondocks; then you'll find something, but the networks, no.

Even the corporations have lessened the number of video communications people that they keep on staff. IBM is a prime example. We are turning more and more to vendors to supply our needs. So I would tell your students, sure, corporate communications is a viable field, but I think you have to try the corporations that are into video, or are thinking about getting into video, and if you have no success there, go beyond the corporations and find the large production companies that are providing services to those corporations. Check the phone listings and find out where they are—these suppliers in New York City, New Jersey, Connecticut—and then start calling or writing letters.

Once you've broken in, once your career is started, the rest should be easy; you'll always work. Corporations are becoming increasingly committed to television.

It seemed to me that this was good sound advice. It was related particularly to opportunities on the East Coast, but I felt that it might be true in any major market where someone might be seeking work in television. Try the networks and the network affiliates as a source of work, but just know that you have other alternatives, corporate communications being one of them. I asked Lloyd if he knew of some companies that were heavily involved in corporate communications.

I know that Sears in Chicago has a vast studio complex and does a lot of video. And up until about a year ago, J. C. Penney was operating heavily out of New York City. They had studios high in an office tower on Sixth Avenue, and they would do weekly broadcasts to all of their stores, showing them what merchandise they should be featuring, sending them bulletins about pricing, etc.

That's where IBM's Field Television Network did its first pilot, and where we continued to feed from until Penney decided to move their whole operation to Dallas. I assume that they are continuing to do as much as they did from there. We've now gone to a company called Unitel in New York City, where they have built a studio for us, a much improved facility, and where we are currently broadcasting.

I know that Citibank produces a lot of videotapes; I found that out through some of our vendors. AT&T has two or three locations in New Jersey, and they are constantly in use. NYNEX is another big user of television. They have a good-sized studio in their building on 42nd Street and Sixth Avenue, and they do a lot of broadcasting. Merrill Lynch is another company that I know of that uses television creatively.

I asked if Lloyd had any idea of specifically how these other companies used video.

Basically marketing support, I think. I believe that's the magical word in corporate communications. Marketing, as you know, is the corporation synonym for sales, and most companies are always trying to find ways in which they can enlarge their customer base, increase their sales, so whatever they can do, they will. A lot of department stores and supermarkets are now using point-of-sale videos, and they've been quite successful in moving merchandise. Well, someone has to produce them, write them and go out and make them, so that's another growing field—the tapes that are being shown in consumer locations.

I told Lloyd that it concerned me a bit that television was going to become a marketing tool and little else. With deregulation, even the number of commercials in programs was becoming excessive. Would that mean the minimization of program content and program values, turning the whole programming day into one big sales tool?

I'm not too happy about it, but I think we've got to have that kind of thing to keep the whole system going. Meanwhile, there are lots of wonderful things available to us, in spite of the commercial world we live in. People have been beating up on commercial television since it began, but somehow or other there are always things to watch, and watch we do, in spite of the commercials. Then, too, there's always PBS, which tries to keep some of the things that we believe in alive. I think there are lots of producers and directors and writers around who have very high standards for their work, whether it be on commercial or public television, and I think they are the people who are going to keep the whole thing going and not let it go down the drain.

I've been at IBM for eighteen years now, and I have no doubt that when

I came to the company, it was the right move for me. At the time I left ABC, in 1970, I remember it as a great time of unrest at the networks. Well, it's not much different today—a little more panic than unrest, perhaps. But, in retrospect, I think your creative juices can flow wherever you hang your hat. This company has tremendous respect for those that they feel can do their jobs well. And in spite of the fact that the bookkeepers have taken over at ABC, I still don't believe that creativity is completely stultified by it. I often see more creativity on something like *Wide World of Sports*, or in the coverage of special events, than I ever thought the company was capable of. I guess what I'm saying is that there are still creative people around and creative situations which support them.

Finally, I asked Lloyd about himself, what he saw for the next five years, the next ten, the next eighteen years.

Well, quite frankly, I would like to get back into that crazy live news orbit once or twice more before I hang it all up. I've been thinking about cutting out of all this as a steady job in another two or three years, when the financial burden of sending two kids through college is completed. I would hope that I could still continue doing some live directing periodically, just to keep my hand in. But as I say, I am intrigued by politics, by elections, by the whole national scene, and I would like to participate in some way or other using my television skills. I find that most gratifying.

8

Larry Auerbach: Directing the Soaps

I am amazed at just how much of television's history has passed through the hands of some of the directors that I have interviewed for this collection. Larry Auerbach is one of them. I always think of TV's year of emergence as 1948. The technology existed before then, and there were notable experiments with the medium, but it wasn't until after World War II, as life slowly came back to normal, that television began its phenomenal growth. So there are men working today, forty years later, vigorous men in their early sixties, like Larry Auerbach, who give great continuity to the events and the programs that have shaped our business.

I talked with Larry in his office at the Director's Guild of America, in the building that the Guild owns on West 57th Street in New York City. The building is in a busy, crowded block that includes, among other things, Carnegie Hall, the Russian Tea Room, and the office of Woody Allen. It's a block that's at the heart of New York show business. Larry has maintained a close connection with the Guild over the years, and in 1989 is its national vice-president and a member of the Council that governs it.

In the quiet of his office, we reminisced about his early days in Chicago, where he had gone to work for NBC, fresh out of the army and with a degree from Northwestern University's School of Speech. He explained that the Speech Department at Northwestern was the educational umbrella for all the theatre and radio activities at the school. No explanation was necessary because mine was a kindred experience, graduating from the University of Illinois Speech Department, and similarly, his break-in job had been in radio, but by

Larry Auerbach (© 1989 CAPITAL CITIES/ABC, INC. [Ann Limongello])

1949, television had grown so quickly that Larry was already working as a director in the NBC studios atop the Merchandise Mart in Chicago.

Those were the palmy days of Chicago television. We had *The Dave Garroway Show,* with Bob Banner directing—Bob was a classmate of mine at Northwestern, as was Dan Petrie, who is a top motion picture director today and started his career in Chicago television. *Mr. Wizard,* with Don Herbert, originated in Chicago. In fact, I put the show on the air; I was its first director and continued to do so until I left. Jules Power, who was another Northwestern graduate, was the producer of *Mr. Wizard.*

We did *Zoo Parade,* the Marlin Perkins show, from Chicago. In fact, we did two *Zoo Parades* every Sunday: one for the NBC network and one for the local station. *Hawkins Falls,* the first television soap opera, was done there. Dan Petrie directed it; I was the stage manager. We did the *Quiz Kids, Stud's Place* with Studs Terkel, *The George Gobel Show.* Clifton Utley was doing the news from Chicago then, and one of his writers was John Chancellor, fresh out of the University of Illinois. Well, I sometimes directed the news, and Jack not only wrote the show, but sometimes stage-managed it. As you know, we both went on from there. Today, one of Jack's colleagues at NBC News is Garrick Utley, who is Clifton's son.

It was a wild and crazy place; I guess we were all very fortunate being in the right spot at the right time.

Larry's series of quick flashbacks almost obscured the fact that he had served a long and productive apprenticeship in his Chicago years, but now I wanted to know how he had made the move to New York, and what had precipitated it.

Well, my family was here. I'm originally from Mt. Vernon, and I had to come back as my father was ill. After the crisis was over, I had no intention of staying on. I had my bag all packed, ready to go back to Chicago. But while I was here, I got a call from Dan Petrie telling me that Roy Windsor was looking for someone to work on a new show called *Love of Life.*

I had known Roy from Chicago, where he had been heavily involved in serials, and I had worked for him on *The Cliff Norton Show.* Roy was now in New York, working as vice-president in charge of television and radio for the Biow Company, a big ad agency. They were about to put two new shows on the air, one was something called *Search for Tomorrow,* which was scheduled to debut on the 3rd of September. The other was *Love of Life,* which was to go on the 24th of September of that same year, 1951.

Well, I went in to see Roy, and he told me that they had already done a couple of pilots on *Love of Life* and that he was not satisfied with what he had seen so far, and he asked me if I would be interested in doing the show. I told him that I would, and he hired me. Well, I put the show on the air on their projected date, the 24th of September, 1951, and I took it off the air in January of 1980, twenty-eight years later.

The show started as fifteen minutes in black and white, then it went to a half-hour in black and white, then to color, which it was when the show was cancelled. We never made it to the hour form; we were cancelled before that became the vogue. Soaps have been good to me; I've done them continuously for 37 years and don't feel like I'm about to quit yet.

I asked Larry if he had done other things besides soaps during that period—I knew that he had because he had worked for me once. I wondered if he found the switch difficult.

Yes, for two reasons. One, I don't like to do half a job, so if I'm doing a soap, especially now that we are working in the hour form, a length which requires a tremendous amount of preparation, it's very difficult to do anything else and still be conscientious about the soap you are doing.

Secondly, as you know, there is a tremendous elitism in our business, which involves a lot of looking down one's nose at the soaps, especially by the people who are doing the prime time shows. The people who do that have no idea of what we do, of the skill it takes, how difficult it is to put together forty-two minutes worth of dramatic air time, each and every day.

One of the main reasons that people minimize the soaps is that they say that nothing happens on the air. Well, a great deal is happening, all of the time—they're just not watching. The shows move very rapidly, and our production values are tremendous, as great as nighttime. We do a lot of location stuff these days, a lot of stunts. It's very different now than it was when we started. But people in the business are still in the habit of saying, "Oh, he's just a soap opera director," and that does mitigate against getting other work.

But then, too, it's partially my own fault. I just don't look for other work. I've been very happy all these years with a regular check coming and, with it, the ability to lead a rather structured life.

I was curious to find out what the nature of that structure was and how it might differ from that of other shows not in the same genre. I questioned him first about those early fifteen-minute broadcasts and then about the half hours: what kind of schedules they operated under, and whether they rehearsed and broadcast in the same day.

If you were on the air live, as we were, across the noon hour, you started your rehearsal on the afternoon of the day before your broadcast. In those three afternoon hours, we did all our blocking and all of the talking that needed to be done: what the scenes were about, why this was happening this way, and how, if anything seemed wrong to us, we could make it work by the following day.

There were no teleprompters. The actors went home and learned their lines overnight. We came in the next morning, had an hour's worth of dry rehearsal, did our blocking, had our dress and then went on camera and did the show. When we went to the half-hour version, I used the same schedule, but at some point in time that all changed. There was a strong movement on the part of AFTRA* to require additional payment if you rehearsed the show on one day and taped it on the next. The actors felt that they were doing two days of work for one day's pay. They also felt that if they were doing a show on a Tuesday and had to stay on for a rehearsal for Wednesday's show, they might miss a commercial audition or something.

I thought it was very shortsighted because I felt then, and still do, that rehearsing the day before gives everyone a chance to sleep on the show, and that helps memory, which helps performance and, most of all, helps me—in ironing out the things that I might be doing badly, in interpretation, in communicating with the actors, in blocking my show.

But the change was made, which I think would have been a disaster, except for the fact that videotape came in, and you didn't have to be finished at the time the show was over, and if you wanted to cover your mistakes, you could, and if you wanted to do something over, you could. You no longer had the same time constraints. The only constraints you had were those imposed upon you by your budget: for example, if you had a studio day of four hours, and you kept going for six, you'd be eating into your budget.

Most of the daytime serials are now on tape, working in a mode that is euphemistically called "live on tape." The directors try and hold to their time limitations, but there is such a large margin for error that they are constantly forced into the editing room: to adjust lapses in memory, to adjust underrehearsed and overproduced fluffs, to keep up with difficult schedules. I asked Larry if he considered *Love of Life* a "live on tape" show.

Not really. The show was taped and then played back two weeks later, so if you had to go and edit, you just went and edited. We do a show today

* The American Federation of Television and Radio Artists, the national union which negotiates the working conditions for actors in television.

that is supposed to be "live on tape," but it's not; it's an edited show. We go in, and we'll do our show, and if somebody fluffs, we'll go back and find a pickup point, or there are times we'll go back to the beginning of the scene. "Live on tape" means something else—that you went from start to finish and you didn't correct anything.

My schedule for *One Life to Live,* on which I am currently working, and all the other shows that I have worked since *Love of Life* went off the air goes something like this: I'm in the studio at 6:30 A.M., and I check the studio and make sure that the props for the various scenes are on hand and that the prop man knows when those props will be used.

I check the sets, and if the furniture's not exactly where I figure it should be, I get the stage hands and get them to push the furniture around. The lighting director is in at that time, and if I am planning any substantial changes in the original lighting plot, I'll let him know at that time.

At 7 A.M. the actors come in, and we start our dry rehearsal in the rehearsal hall. We rehearse until 9:45. Now, most of the actors haven't learned their lines yet. No fault of theirs—some of them have been on the show the day before, or two consecutive days, or three days before. Sometimes the writers write them in for five, six, seven, eight days in a row. It's an exhausting routine for an actor—very pressured. Then, too, we no longer use teleprompters on the show. I didn't think that was going to work at first, but it has, much better than I thought it would.

We got rid of the prompters because the producers got tired of seeing people look at them. Now, there's no backup, and the actors have to memorize, and they usually do.

Anyway, I come into that 7 A.M. dry rehearsal with a completely marked script. I have not seen the show in rehearsal, so I have to sit at home, by myself, and block the script in my head. Not just with regard to cameras, but with regard to the actors—you don't do one without the other. That's why I felt that having rehearsal on the day before was better. Then my concentration could be on performance, not the blocking, and only then can you make your cameras photograph what organically belongs to the actors. The other puts the cart before the horse.

Fortunately, I've been doing it for so long, that if I discover that something doesn't work, I can change the cameras to accommodate the acting, rather than having to force the actors into positions that work for camera. Sometimes, though, you have to do that; there isn't enough time to make the mechanical changes necessary, so you just say to the performer, "Hey, that's the way it is, and that's the way you have to do it."

I think one of the hallmarks of a good director is the ability to block things in your head as you are reading a script—or even more, when you are working on location, whether with a single camera or multiple ones, seeing images in your mind as you shoot, knowing how they will cut. Needless to say, it's wiser to rehearse, if you can, but when a situation closes out on you as it sometimes does for Larry Auerbach, then you must go into this kind of blind blocking. Like Larry, I feel that this is a tremendous disadvantage for performers because they become so preoccupied with their physical performance—just the chore of getting their lines right takes almost all the concentration that they can give and makes it very difficult for the actor to reach any kind of emotional level.

I proceeded now to go back to Larry's studio schedule. After the dry blocking in the rehearsal hall, I asked what happened next. I wondered when he had time for notes and time to help the actors with their performances.

Well, it depends on whom you are working with. Most of the performers, especially the ones with long runs on long-running soaps, have been doing their parts for years—they know their characters inside out, backwards and forward, and even more, they've been working with some of the same actors for years, so it's really like an ensemble company. It's not like they're coming in and picking up a piece of material for the first time, so with the exception of certain refinements, you really don't have to get into every little bit and piece of action. If you come to a scene that may be critical, that may be one that you'll want to give some additional time to.

For new performers, or young performers—and they're not necessarily the same—I try and take a few moments with them during the morning blocking, explain what the scene's about, what's been going on before their arrival on the scene, what we are looking for in their character. I try to get them to understand the mechanics of how the show works.

Specific notes with regard to that day's performance can really only be given at the note session, which comes after dress and before we tape.

Now, as I said earlier, most of the performers come into rehearsal without having learned their lines fully. They learn them as we do them, during the day. We do anywhere from 95 to 100 pages a day. Not everyone is in every scene, but it's not unusual for somebody to have 40 or 50 pages to do, and 20 to 30 pages is fairly standard. And these people are just extraordinary. They do learn their lines. It seems that their memorization capabilities expand the more they do the show.

After we finish our dry rehearsal at 9:45, there's a short break of fifteen minutes, and I usually go back into the studio again to check on my crew. The technicians have come in by that time, and I want to see who's going to be on camera that day. We start camera blocking at 10 o'clock and block from 10 to 12:30; then we break for lunch, come back at a quarter to 2 and do a dress rehearsal until about a quarter of 4. Then I give the cast and crew my notes.

I like to give my notes on the set; most of the other directors do them in the makeup room. I was just brought up that way, giving them on the set. I think it works better that way, allows the actors to visualize the changes a little better.

We start taping, hopefully, by 4:30, and if the show is a normal kind of show, without too many flourishes, we can figure on being done by 6:30 or 7. Then everybody goes away and comes back the next morning to start all over again—it's a tough routine.

Now, because of this kind of demanding routine, and the fact that each show requires a tremendous amount of preparation by the director, we have a group of directors who work the show. No one director could do five of these in one week. Even with my background it takes me 10 to 12 hours to prepare a script, and I don't like to do that in one day. I try and spread it out over two and even three days if I can.

So, I generally do two shows one week and one in the next—that's my schedule. And we have three other fine directors doing the same. Peter Minor, who was a CBS A.D. for many years, does two and one as I do. David Pressman, who has been around for a long while, does one a week, and Gary Bowen, who came to us from California, where he was also a CBS A.D., does one a week. It takes four of us to make a week of *One Life to Live* work, the demands of getting the show done are so heavy.

There's one other part of the routine which I neglected to tell you about, and that's the tech meeting which takes place on the day before you do your show. We have two lighting directors that work the show and two T.D.s, all of whom alternate. The director of Wednesday's show meets on Tuesday with the lighting director and the technical director who will work with him on his show day. So I come into that tech meeting with all of my lighting and all of my performance positions indicated on a floor plan, and I go over all of the following day's positions and movements with both of these men and discuss any of the problems that I might foresee in the upcoming show.

But our preparation goes back even further than that. We have a production meeting for all five shows in a given week that takes place ten days prior to the Monday that the week starts. At that meeting each director sits there surrounded by a large group of people—the associate producers, the scenic designer, a person from the lighting department, the people from production services (there's at least thirty people in that meeting)—and goes over the proposed floor plan that the designer has come up with, seeing what problems we might have to face and how we can solve them.

You can't help but be impressed by the complexity and the amount of pre-production that goes into the making of a soap. I'm a great believer in the "all things happen in pre-production" school of television—that if you work carefully and pay attention to detail *before* you go into the studio, there's not too much that can go wrong. But preplanning also meaning that your script must be there on time. I asked Larry when he saw his script for the first time.

I just received my script today for a show that's scheduled in three weeks. But there are times that I will get them even earlier than that. Those are so-called "unedited scripts." They come to me at the same time they go to the story editors, who work with the writers. I prefer to work from the unedited script rather than the edited version because it gives me a few extra days to look at it, without waiting for the editors.

When I get the script, the first thing I do is make out a taping schedule. This is an important consideration on my show because we do not do the show consecutively, from page 1 to page 100; we break it up, depending on locations and costume changes. For example, we will do all the scenes on one set, whatever their order, finish there and then go on to another set. By careful scheduling, this permits some of the actors to get out a little early, not have to wait around until the last minute if they are in one of the later scenes.

It's a little bit of a logistical nightmare figuring it all out, but I like to do it myself because it gives me a better understanding of what the flow of the show is going to be.

Through the courtesy of Sid Kerner, one of the technicians on *One Life to Live* and an old friend, I was able, over the years I was teaching, to bring my graduate interns from Brooklyn College to the studio. It was a tremendous learning experience for them—and even more for me. I had been in the director's chair only once for a soap and was a bit thrown by the pace and involvement of the job. Seeing it from the studio floor, I was overwhelmed by the intricacy of it all. One of the stage managers described it as "a 24-hour-a-day operation." I asked Larry if he would describe some of the behind-the-scenes operations of the show for me.

On a normal day, we always have six or seven sets standing. Most of them are the sets that are going to work on the show that day. Now, if by some chance we use only four or five of those sets on Tuesday, let us say, and there is a set that was up on Monday, which won't work Tuesday, but will be used on Wednesday, they might leave that set standing. Normally, if six or seven sets are standing, some of them will be struck every night and new ones put up. If they all go down, it's called a complete wipeout.

Anyway, let's say that's what we have, a complete wipeout. Whenever we finish, regardless of how early or late, the stage crew strikes the sets, and trucking comes in with the new sets. We have three separate crews of stage hands that work the show, incidentally. So the old sets are struck and run onto the loading ramp, and the new scenery is brought in, and the setup begins. They start to light at around 3 A.M., and that's another reason why we have alternate lighting directors; that lighting director is there from setup to the completion of your taping, and it doesn't make any difference if you finish at 6:30 or at midnight.

As the stage hands are setting the show, the lighting director works behind them, working from the floor plan that I have given him the previous day at our tech meeting.

Once the carpenters have put the final nails into the sets, the sets are propped. The prop department comes in with all the final touches: the couches, the chairs, the tables, plus all the hand props that might be called for in that day's shoot. And by this time, I should be able to start blocking on the floor.

Up until this point in time, I had always assumed that I could recognize the work of certain directors as viewed on the home screen. But in this case, I wasn't sure that such virtuosity was a plus. After all, you were doing continuing episodes of the same story, and a great variety in the look of succeeding days was not something to be wished for. I questioned Larry about the difficulty of maintaining a unanimity of look and performance with different directors at the helm.

Each director has a unique approach to the material, to the way he shoots it, puts it together, but you also have a producer who sits in the control room when you are doing your dress and provides a third eye, which to a certain extent can help smooth out those differences. The performers are also a great help. They know their characters as well as anyone can, and they also remember the continuity of the characters. These things all help to smooth out what might be differences in a day's work. So far as the directors are concerned, all of us have worked together long enough, and seen each other's work often enough, that there is an overall sameness to the week. I don't think that anyone in the audience can tell when my work is up on the screen, or if it's Peter's.

I persisted. I asked Larry if there is nothing in his particular style that's different from that of the other directors on *One Life to Live*.

I would be hard pressed to be able to tell you. I do try and use a lot of movement. I do try and stay over the shoulder a lot. I do so because I have strong feelings about involving the audience as much as I can, and I do this by staying over the shoulder of the other participant in the scene, the person who is not speaking at the moment, the person who may just be reacting. As a result, the audience is not out front as a spectator, but within the scene. In a sense, they become the person over whose shoulder I am shooting.

And as time has gone by, I find myself less and less addicted to a great number of close-ups that we used in those early days of television, and I've thought about it a lot: why we did it then, why I'm not doing it now. For one thing, watching that small set in your living room years ago, I think there was a curious kind of optical thing that occurred. It wasn't like the theatre, where you sat in a half-lit house, watching the stage, not aware of anything around you, and so, as you watched the play, your mind's eye made those people in the play life-size because you saw them in relationship to everything else on the stage—the furniture, the props—all of which your mind made to seem life-size.

Now, if you sat in your living room watching the small screen, and it was daytime, or the room was lit, there was a difference, especially if the director was shooting his people full-sized, or even three-quarter size. Everyone on the screen then became infinitesimal as compared to the furniture around them, of which the viewers were always subconsciously aware. So, it became important to command the attention of the home audience by having really big faces on the screen. Hence, a lot of close-ups.

Today, it's not as important. The sets are larger and more sophisticated. The screens are larger, and technically, we're putting out a better picture with better lighting. So, I have been trying to get away from close-up, close-up, close-up.

The one thing that always impressed me about Larry was how quickly he worked. I once hired him to direct a show for me, and I think that was the sole reason I did—the speed with which he worked. That he also directed brilliantly was a pleasant plus as a result of his engagement. It was an interesting project, and worth recounting for this text. I think it was one of the first programs ever purchased for cable television. The California company owned by ex-NBC president Pat Weaver (which was later legislated off the airwaves after an intensive lobbying campaign by West Coast movie theatre owners) had commissioned Ted Mann, the managing director of the Circle-in-the-Square Off-Broadway Theatre Company, to produce one of their plays for television. The play was Bill Ball's production of Pirandello's *Six Characters in Search of an Author*, which was currently playing at the Martinique Theatre under Circle-in-the-Square's production auspices.

Ted had signed a contract to deliver the play on tape for a certain price, but as he began to examine his deal, he discovered that there was no way he could do so. I was just fresh from my two years of producing *The Play of the Week,* and Ted called me and promised me a quite decent fee if I could bring the show in under a certain figure that would still give him a profit. I, in turn, called Larry Auerbach.

It was a tough day, Jack. That was a tough, tough show to do. As I remember, we taped it from the stage of the Martinique Theatre, which was built into an old ballroom. The Martinique has now become a welfare hotel, and none of that exists any more, I'm sure.

We are lucky that the show had been playing for some time, so everyone was well rehearsed. Paul Shenar was in the play; Jacqueline Brooks, who's a wonderful actress, was in it; Richard Dysart, who now stars in *L.A. Law,* was in it. It was a great company as I remember, and it was all done on a thrust stage that was little more than a couple of platforms extending into the audience—no curtain or anything. The stage was surrounded on three sides by the ticket holders.

We had a pickup crew from all three networks, and we worked from a remote truck that was owned and run by Hank Alexander, who was a lighting director for CBS. Everyone was moonlighting. The truck was a monster, compared to the relatively small units that we use today. And then when you saw what we had to use for equipment, it was a shocker.

As I remember it, there were two terrible things that happened on that shoot. One, it was an extremely hot day—so much so that we had to keep the equipment in the truck to prevent it from overheating. There just wasn't enough power in the theatre to supply the amount of power needed for air conditioning in the Martinique and in the truck.

So the poor actors were dying, and we rehearsed all afternoon; we were trying to do the whole thing in one taping day. It was a complicated play, with lots of exits and entrances, almost all of them from the audience. It wasn't a proscenium piece by any means, and there was just no place to hide. If I recall, we had five cameras placed in the audience. We had to pull out several rows of seats in order to find room for the cameras.

The other terrible thing that happened was that we had hired an audio man who had never been out in the field before and was not exactly proficient at this kind of thing—doing plays on location. This audio man was a lovely guy; I knew him from CBS, but his only experience was in the studio, and we had no body mikes in those days.

He came and saw the show on the night before we taped and said that we might have some trouble getting a good pickup from the thrust stage, as it was built over a hollow platform. When we started to tape, there was a lot of movement, and we couldn't hear a damn thing. So, in the middle of the day—I don't know if you remember this—we took a break, got some guys from some kind of insulation place, who crawled in under the platform on that hot day, and stapled fiberglass or rock wool on the underside of that stage to deaden the sound.

It was a tremendous undertaking—to try and do that play with no prior rehearsal. I had big cards made up, if you recall, for the actors to wear during their first run-through, so that the cameramen could identify which character they were shooting. Then, too, we had cameramen from three different networks who were accustomed to two different working styles, so that was a bit of a problem.

In addition, I had an A.D. who was supposed to meet me on the night before we taped and take my script so he could prepare a script for himself, and he never showed up—he had been at a wedding and drank a little too much. So he was behind me all day long, instead of ahead of me.

And finally, when we let the audience in, we discovered that they had sold the seats that we had taken out of the theatre for the cameras, and there was a little bit of a riot by the people who couldn't get in.

It was all very, very difficult, working that quickly, under those conditions, but it got done, didn't it?

I had not remembered most of the things that Larry told me about, although I was there all through the taping day. I do remember, however, that it was a very successful show, and Ted Mann was delighted that we had brought the show in under his budget figure. There is a psychological principle that says we fortunately remember only the pleasanter aspects of situations. Well, in this case, it was certainly true for me because I did remember the terrific job that Larry had done in holding it all together and shooting the show. I knew the answer to the question, but I asked it anyway: Working quickly doesn't necessarily mean that you sacrifice quality, does it?

If it did, I don't think I'd be here today. There are sacrifices that have to be made in every performance medium. If we didn't make them, I guess we would all be able to turn out perfect work every time—but at tremendous cost. So working quickly really means that you do your best within the limits of the dollars and the hours that you have available to you, and if you can't do that and meet the need for a certain standard of quality, you don't work.

And I think that's truer today than ever before. We're in a bottom-line kind of business now, where costs are all-important, and everyone has to adjust his working schedule so that he or she works well and, somehow or other, maintains quality.

I asked him what some of the things are that he does as the pace quickens and he strives for quality. Is there any time for setting up shots just for the sheer beauty of them? Is there any time for doing things that are aesthetically pleasing?

If I am able to communicate to the audience through the camera's eye a performance that's interesting, or exciting, or stimulating—it seems to me that's a form of aesthetics.

I personally don't care to do a show in which I demonstrate my ability to get a beautiful shot when that shot is going to call attention to itself and, as a result, take the audience away from the performance.

For example: two young lovers are lying in front of a fireplace. You can go around behind the fireplace, remove the backing and shoot through the fireplace and get the fire in the foreground. It's a cliché shot, one that I personally would never take, because the minute you do that, you break the audience's concentration on what you are paid to make them concentrate on: the characters and the story.

So, although I enjoy getting the camera to move, and do so all of the time, I also enjoy getting everything on the show to look clean and well shot. I don't like setup shots, something that says, "Oh, look, the flowers are right there in the foreground, and that's significant." That's not significant of anything, except an ego trip. So I only have time to make the work accomplish what I want it to accomplish, which is to involve the audience in the story and with the characters.

I have always had great compassion for the people who work on the soaps, in spite of the fact that I am not a viewer. It's a much maligned form; everybody dumps on the soaps. But every time I meet someone who works them, both behind the camera and on, I am always aware of how conscientious and dedicated these people who work the daytime serials are. I asked Larry if there ever were attitude problems or cynicism about content on the shows he had worked.

Directing a soap is a very demanding job, and you have to give it your full attention, or you can't do it properly, and if you have no respect for the job, you wind up having no respect for yourself.

The performers on the shows work very hard at them. They'll occasionally bitch about the scripts, but so do I. You'll hear me say some terrible things about some of our scripts, but that only comes out of a strong desire to want to do better, to want to have more. We try to do the best we can with what we have. And that's certainly true of the writers. It seems to me that writing a daily soap opera is just about the hardest job that a writer can have—just turning out that tremendous amount of material must be mind-blowing. Do you realize what a hundred pages of script a day means? 500 pages a week, 52 weeks a year, 260 shows, 260 times a hundred is 26,000 pages of script a year. Writing all that is tough, tough work. Not just creating the dialogue, but planning the stories, plotting them—those people deserve a lot of credit.

There was a time when I used to get involved with the scripts, much more involved than I do now. In fact, before the network took over *Love of Life* around 1969, I used to work with producers on the script, sat in on story conferences, was much more responsible for casting. When CBS took over the production of *Life* and *Secret Storm* from Roy Windsor Productions, most of that involvement disappeared.

Today, with three or four directors on the show, an executive producer, a producer, a head writer and sub-writers, two casting people—there's no room for the directors to get involved in script and casting. We're just so busy getting the material out, there's little room for anything else.

Now, if we get a script and we feel that there have to be changes, we can go to the producer and the writer and say, "Look, this doesn't work," and maybe we'll get a change; maybe we won't. We do have some leeway when it comes to changing lines, and I've always felt very strongly that a director has to have that right—to change lines. If it's easier for an actor to communicate an idea with different words, that's okay with me, but we can't change the ideas. I think there we have an obligation to the writer, especially if that change might affect the whole story line down the road.

I still wanted Larry to tell us more about the huge ABC studio where *One Life to Live* is taped: a long rectangle with multiple sets lining the two long walls of the studio. There was an aisle down the middle from which the directors worked their cameras and their booms. It struck me as a very difficult kind of blocking job.

As you say, the sets are lined up from one end of the studio to the other, along the long walls. Only the middle of the studio is left free, so you can run your cameras and lights from the fronts of those sets. In order to keep us from getting tangled up in the spaghetti from the camera cables, and still have some kind of mobility, we have one camera come out of each of the short ends of the studio, and a camera that comes out of each of the long walls of the studio. So we have four cameras, one coming out from each wall.

When I sit down and work my floor plan, I have to know where my cameras come from. If I am working a set at the very end of the studio, Camera One is on my left, Camera Four might be in the middle and Camera Two on my right; then if I go to the other end, it might be Camera Three on the left, Camera Two in the middle and Camera Four on the right.

Sounds a bit confusing, I know, but the important thing is that you have to know where your cables are coming from, and then you just lay it all out.

We have one innovative thing on the studio floor, something fairly unusual, which we call "the podium." When I was working the half-hour shows at CBS, I did all my camera blocking from the control room. It was effective because I could see all three monitors at once and know what was on all three cameras, but it was inefficient in terms of the time we had to rehearse, especially if I had to get up and run out in the studio, adjust an actor's position, or talk to one of the cameramen about where he should be. I felt that I spent far too much time tracking back and forth between the studio and the control room.

On the hour shows it's even worse—we don't have any spare time. Our blocking time is only slightly more than we had when we were doing the half-hour shows.

Anyway, when I did *All My Children* at CBS, the producer was a wonderful guy by the name of Jørn Winter—that's Jørn with a slash through the "o"—Jørn was Danish. He was also a director, and prior to his coming to *All My Children,* the directors on the show stayed on the floor, watching monitors that were mounted on the grid, calling directions through a headset to the control room where the technical director took the shots from a previously marked script.

It was a very inefficient way to work, and Jørn hated it, so he developed a rolling stand that had a very small monitor, a microphone, and a playback speaker built into it. He could hear the control room on the little speaker, talk to control or the cameramen. Yet he could still stand there, in view of the set and what was going on in the studio, checking his picture on the monitor.

When I moved over from *All My Children* to *One Life to Live,* one of the few things that I asked them to do for me was build me a podium! It has since been refined somewhat, so that we no longer have to use the microphone and the speaker. We wear an earpiece and have an RF mike, so we can communicate from anywhere on the studio floor. I don't really like directing from the studio floor, but in my estimation it's absolutely necessary on the hour shows. You just don't have time to run in and out of the control room.

I was winding down the interview with Larry Auerbach, and there were still many areas that I felt I hadn't covered. For one thing, I wanted to ask about the new morality in television, where the "soaps" seemed to be in the forefront of a new standard of behavior. I asked him if the soaps' current preoccupation with sex presented any problems. His immediate answer was, "For whom?" I, of course, replied, "For you, as a director." We both laughed, and he went on to give me a serious answer.

Well, there is a standards and practices department at ABC, which reads all the scripts, and says, "Please make sure that this scene is executed in good taste." But the question of good taste is a subjective one; I am certainly not in the business of making porno movies.

There's no question about the fact that there is more sex, or at least a freer portrayal of sexual liaisons on the soaps today than there was ten years ago, but I think that's a reflection of the society that we live in. We deal more freely with sex in our movies, we deal more freely with sex in our publications, we deal more freely with sex in our personal relationships.

The soaps are both a mirror and a leader in presenting a portrait of the contemporary mores and customs of a certain segment of our society. They're a reflection of what's going on today. I don't think that the shows are dramatically any richer than the behavior that you find in real life. Maybe, but just maybe, our programs expose a more advanced point of view to certain sections of this country where life isn't—how can I say this?—that free.

I must admit that there are times when I've felt that a scene shouldn't have been shot or shown, and if I did, I would go and talk to the producer or the writer, and if they felt that it was essential to the story line, I had two alternatives: I could do it, or I could go away. It may come as a surprise to some people, but directing soaps is like anything else; it's a business where you get paid to do a job. So if I'm going to take the check at the end of the week, after I've told them what I think, and I've told them why it's wrong for us to do something, or bad for us to do it, or damaging to the show to do it, and they say, "Okay, do it anyway," then that decision has become theirs, and I'm left with the decision as to whether the problem is something I want to walk away from.

In the old days we used to do live commercials, and I was frequently hired to do them. I would come in and show the people from the advertising agency how I wanted to shoot the commercial, but if they wanted to shoot it another way, that was up to them, since they were paying me. If they chose not to use my experience, my expertise, my professional skills, I would think that they were very foolish, and often as not, they didn't. So I either walked, or I did it their way as well as I could. That's the key: if you decide to do something, the important thing is to do it as well as you can.

I reminded Larry that he promised to tell me a couple of talent stories, tales of young actors who started on the soaps and went on to become stars in Hollywood or the stars who become intrigued with the soaps and agreed to make cameo appearances.

There are a lot of people that have supported themselves by working on the soaps at some point in their career, for a greater or lesser period of time. Warren Beatty, for example, appeared for a while on *Love of Life,* shortly after he graduated from Northwestern, but that was a long time ago.

I was at the annual convention of the Director's Guild a year ago this past June, a meeting at which we elected new officers and conducted our business, and as you know, Warren is now a member, and a very active one, and he was sitting directly behind me, and I didn't say anything to him. I really didn't think he would remember me. Anyway, I was introduced as being one of the officers of the Guild, and when there was a break in the proceedings, Warren leaned forward, tapped me on the shoulder, and introduced himself, and said, "I don't know if you remember me, but I once worked for you on *Love of Life.*"

Roy Scheider also worked on *Love of Life,* as well as *Secret Storm.* Burt Convy, whom I think everyone knows as a game show host, worked on *Love of Life* for a long time. He played a masked intruder, a molester of teen-age girls, and the girl that he molested was Bonnie Bedelia, who also worked for us. I saw her recently in a movie called *Die Hard,* and she was just splendid in it. I know that Hal Halbrook worked on a soap for a long time. Who else? Jessica Walter worked on *Love of Life* for a long period and has always been very giving, saying what a rewarding experience it was to have worked on our show.

And, of course, Elizabeth Taylor came on *All My Children,* shortly after I left, but Carol Burnett was there while I was, for a brief appearance, and she was absolutely wonderful. Sammy Davis, Jr., is a great fan of the soaps and has made a number of appearances. There are any number of people who started their careers, making a living, sharpening their skills, by working on soaps.

I got a sense of great fulfillment from what he does as I talked to Larry Auerbach: I had a feeling that he was someone who really puts his heart and soul into what he does, does it well, and gets a great sense of satisfaction from it. I wondered if he ever had the desire now, late in his career, to do other things, to get involved in one of the nighttime soaps, for example, like *Dallas,* or *Dynasty,* or *Falcon Crest*—things which I am sure he could do magnificently.

I'm confident that I could, but I have no great desire to go out and make a pitch for them. If somebody came to me, and said, "We'd like you to come out to the Coast and do so-and-so," I'd probably jump at the chance, but I think the days when I was hoping somebody might come and do that are gone. I still think that there is a feeling in the business that exists about daytime soap operas and their directors, and that's what I am, and always have been—a soap opera director.

So I would think that lightning is not going to strike, and I am quite content doing what I am doing, and doing it well. I have no desire to drive myself crazy thinking about the things that I could do; I'm happy doing what I do. I think that I'm appreciated by the people who hire me, and I'm not that anxious to work for people who are going to "give me a chance."

Emily Squires with two of the Muppets.

☆ **9**

Emily Squires: Directing
Sesame Street

Emily Squires strikes me as a very gentle person. A native of Virginia, she went to Randolph-Macon Woman's College in Lynchburg for two years and graduated from the University of North Carolina in Chapel Hill. She wears her southern manners and gentility with great grace. Her behavior in the studio is impeccable. She is most amiable with her crew and her fellow studio workers. Although she does regularly, I'm sure, I cannot envision a situation that would cause Emily to lose her temper. I have often been aware of a certain disparity in the behavior of some of the directors that I have known and worked with between the person they are and the persona that they affect in the studio. I'm afraid that one or two of them can be bastards in the control room and pussycats when you meet them on the street. There is nothing anachronistic about Emily. I am positive that she brushes her teeth with the same equanimity that she possesses in the studio.

After visiting the set of *Sesame Street,* I was invited for afternoon tea with Emily in her large apartment on the upper west side of Manhattan, a step or two away from a busy Broadway intersection. It's an apartment that she shares with a friend of many years, and the first question that I wanted to ask her was if she was married, but I quickly changed my mind. After all, it was none of my business, and certainly not something that I would have asked a man in a similar situation. I was determined that I wasn't going to let any sexism show.

What I really wanted to ask had to do with something I had been thinking about from the first moment that I had started to conduct my interviews, and that was the appalling state of women in New

York television. There are lots of women around, capable ones playing all sorts of important and relevant roles in television, but less than 2 percent of them, as listed in the membership roster of the Director's Guild of America, actively sit in a director's chair in a control room. Emily Squires is one of them, and that was the first thing that I wanted to ask her: What did she think was the reason?

I think it's more than just the directorial profession; I think it's the way of the world in general, the way things are—I truly do. Then, too, as far as television is concerned, I think it's a profession that has a very heavy technical orientation, and traditionally more men than women have sought out this kind of work. Just look around you when you go into the studio: the crews on the studio floor are all male—the boom operators, the cameramen, the prop guys—they're all men.

I asked her if she was suggesting that women can't handle the technical side of television as well as men can. And if so, wouldn't that give the lie to the whole women's revolution of the past twenty years—the women who are carpenters, electricians, telephone installers, even garbage collectors.

I'm not denying that. I'm just saying that it's not a standard, not a normal way for women in television to go, not a career track for them—it's against the grain. The way I came up was much more normal—for a woman. I came up through the ranks, from a production assistant, to an A.D., and finally, after many years, to a director. Most women won't wait it out: they marry or go off and do something else. Men move a lot easier on their career track, so most women just don't think of becoming directors, and it has become almost completely male dominated.

I told Emily that I had theorized through most of my interviews that a finely developed sense of aesthetics would take someone further in television than all the technical training in the world, and she agreed with me. But when I suggested that women have a more finely developed aesthetic sense than men, she demurred. I noted that many men are embarrassed by aesthetic decisions—the decoration of their house, the selection and preparation of food, the purchase and arrangement of flowers—that these decisions are made by women in the household. Women seem to have that aesthetic sense, and men don't—so why not television direction as a career?

I think you've changed the thrust of your question. What I was referring to initially was purely dealing with the road to a career. When you are talking about having the right instincts, or the right eye for making pictures, I think women do have that. On *Sesame Street,* for example, I think that my strengths are on the softer side: dealing with interpersonal relationships, the delicate balance between men and women, a real sensitivity toward children—all of this.

On the other hand, Jon Stone, who is one of the creative forces behind *Sesame Street,* and a fine director himself, is just terrific with puppets and has the ability to make the big joke pay off.

But as I said, when it comes to the sensitive side, I think that I'm just as good as anybody, and I believe that a lot of that has to do with my being a woman.

I commented that perhaps *Sesame Street* was the exception that proved the rule. From my perception it seemed to me to be a show run by women, with men in a secondary role. The parent company, the Children's Television Workshop, was founded and is still being run by a woman, Joan Ganz Cooney. On the day I visited the show, there were only two men in the control room, besides myself, and they were the T.D. and the man in charge of post-production. All the rest were women: the writers, the producer Lisa Simon, associates, production people of all kinds—all women. I asked if they were there because they are more sensitive to the needs and concerns of children than men are.

That's an interesting question, and I would answer, "Yes, it is quite possible true." There are a great many women in children's television—however, few directors. The same is true in daytime television. There are a lot of women in the soap operas as well—and, once again, only a few directors. Maybe it's because the men gravitate to the big bucks of prime time that there is room for lots of women in the daytime.

The fact is that when *Sesame Street* started, there were a great many men working on the shows. Over the twenty years that it has been in production, perhaps the behind-the-scenes gender of the show has changed somewhat, but I would think that part of that has to be that the world has changed, too.

In our pre-interview conversations, Emily had told me that she was an English major in college and thought of herself as a writer. I asked her how she got sidetracked into a career in television.

When I first came to New York, I worked as an editorial assistant in a publishing house, and they paid you no money and wanted you to sweep up afterwards—it was just unbelievable, and to top it off, it was boring.

It just wasn't what I had in my mind for my life, what I wanted to do. So I quit, and I walked into the CBS Personnel Department one spring afternoon and said, "I wanted a job, any kind of job, except a secretarial one!" And I was hired that day, as a secretary, in the news room, working in television—it just happened, and I thought it was all so glamorous. I guess what I was looking for was exactly what everyone else looks for when they come to New York: the excitement and glitz of the city. Now, after twenty years, I'm not so sure that what I was looking for even exists.

Well, it was the most exciting job that I have ever had, working in that network news room. I got to know Walter Cronkite, and Eric Sevareid, and Charles Kuralt, all those wonderful people from when CBS was the ultimate in a news organization. I spent two years there, two wonderful years. Then Av Westin, who was a producer at CBS News, was approached by the Ford Foundation to found something that was to be called the Public Broadcast Laboratory, and he was given a grant of ten million dollars to do so. Well, my boss at the time was a man named Gerry Slater, and Av asked him if he would join him, and Gerry asked me, and I went. Gerry became one of the top people at PBL, and I became his assistant.

What we did at PBL was shape the concept of what was to become the entire PBS network, but produced only one magazine concept show—but I think that was the precursor of most of the magazine formats that you see on the air now, like *60 Minutes, 20/20* and *West 57th Street.* It was a wonderful experience for me, but it lasted for only two years, and when the Ford funding ran out, I needed a job. *Sesame Street* was starting up just about that time, and it was also scheduled for public television, so two of us—Dulcy Singer, who is now the executive producer of the show, and I—left to join *Sesame Street.*

My first job there was as a production assistant, but I eventually became the assistant to the producer and then, over the years, moved into the control room to become an associate director, and then eventually became a director on the show. I had a lot of on-the-job training and was fairly good about absorbing all there was to know. I guess that's true of most of the people who have been with *Sesame Street* for a long time. Very few of them were originally involved in the field of children's education or in creating programs for children. Most of them were generalists like I was and very successful at making the transition.

Emily Squires has remained with *Sesame Street* for twenty years. The first ten of those she was on staff; the next ten she was contracted as a free-lance director for the show. It's a long run for anyone in our business. I asked Emily if *Sesame Street* was her first directorial assignment.

Yes, it was, and it was horrifying. I couldn't sleep for weeks knowing that I was going to do the show, going to actually direct. I wish they hadn't told me that much in advance that I had the assignment, but things can't work logistically unless everyone knows their assignments, so you find out a month in advance, and you have that long for your knees to quake.

I can only guess that Dulcy Singer was responsible for my getting the assignment. You remember, she was the woman who came over with me from PBL. Well, she's been a wonderful friend—she's really been responsible for most of my moves. Luckily, she's always been a step or two ahead of me in the *Sesame Street* hierarchy and has always been very helpful.

Bob Myhrum was also very helpful. I think you told me that you knew Bob quite well at one time. He was one of the first directors on *Sesame Street,* and he was very supportive of the move to make me a director; I had been his associate director for a long time. I learned a lot from Bob. He could be very gruff and very difficult at times, but he sure did know how to work. With Bob, we would get out of the studio at 2 or 3 in the afternoon. With most of the other directors, it would take until 6 to finish.

That was one important thing that I learned from Bob: how to work quickly and well. You knew who was the boss when Bob was in the control room. He ran the place with an iron hand; he knew what he wanted, and people hopped to his drum beat. I learned that from Bob—how to be in charge.

I learned one other thing, too. He was also very conversant with the shooting side of television, and he insisted that I, too, learn what the camera could do. Jon Stone, whom I also assisted for a long time, was more involved with the editorial side, so I really learned from two men with two distinct approaches—two distinct and different directors—and I think I had a really good television education.

The two men that Emily had mentioned had been the prime directors of *Sesame Street* all through its early years. Emily Squires became the first woman to enter into the picture. I asked her if her directorial debut had been a successful one and if the producers of the show continued to let her direct after that.

I guess it was because they continued to let me do the show occasionally, very occasionally, which was terrible, really. But no one ever really said anything to me—good or bad. It would seem to me, if you ever really have a chance to direct something, you should demand a little bit of continuity in your work. How can anyone tell how skilled you are by giving you just one shot at something? What if you were unduly nervous, as I was? You need a transition period as you begin to direct. Even if you know what has to be done, it just takes a while for those things to sink in, so how can anyone tell anything by giving you just one shot at something? How they could figure from that first exposure that I was capable of doing the show, I haven't the vaguest idea.

But I continued to direct, slowly at first, very slowly. In my first year, there were only two days in which they would let me direct, but everyone was very supportive, and very helpful, and over the years my number of engagements began to grow.

We were conducting the interview in Emily's study, where, on the wall, Emily had posted the certificates from the Academy of Television Arts and Sciences that notified her that she had received awards and nominations for her work as a director on *Sesame Street*—awards that would entitle her to an Emmy, the prestigious statuette awarded by the Academy for excellence in television. I told her that it was a very impressive lineup and that the number of her "engagements" certainly must have grown by leaps and bounds to be the recipient of those honors. She minimized her personal accomplishments.

Well, I can't take complete responsibility for those. I really don't know how to characterize them because they are mainly for the show, and I was just one of a group of directors. So I mean it's really a group effort.

I told her that I thought her modesty was very becoming, but I wouldn't accept it. When she persisted and waved me off with a toss of her hand, I told her that all I could see was her name on the award, and that's something I certainly would be proud of. (In fact, I tell everybody about my five Emmys all the time.)

But then I asked her when she really began to feel her oats as a director. I wondered what her first assignment outside of *Sesame Street* was.

After the first year or two, when I began to work fairly regularly on the show, I relaxed and became very comfortable in the control room. And that's the way I am now; I rarely panic. Directing has become almost second nature to me.

As far as outside work is concerned—gee, I've done so many things, for cable, for syndication, for PBS. I've just finished a home video for the Muppets; I've done a lot of things for Jim Henson, outside of *Sesame Street*. I've had a couple of shots on *Search for Tomorrow*, which I may just try and pursue, see if I can do some more. But it's such a hard day doing a soap; it's more like being a traffic cop than being a director. I can't conceive of anything that is more difficult for a director. But you feel that you should do them—but then as you do, you start to wonder, "Is this going to lead to anything?" I know that's a terrible way of looking at things, but if you're going to put yourself through that soap routine, that terrible schedule—you really have to look down the line. And for the longest period of time I didn't think that I did. I thought that being a soap opera director wouldn't lead to anything.

But recently a couple of people have made the switch to nighttime. A couple of soap opera directors that I know have moved to the Coast and are working out there. One, John Whitesell, recently did a *Tattinger's*, a new nighttime show about a restaurant, and he also did a couple of sitcoms—he's slowly breaking through. So I guess it is a way of moving up, and that's given me some second thoughts about directing on the soaps.

I wanted to get back to some of the problems that Emily might have had as a woman breaking into what has always been primarily a man's domain. She told me one story in our preliminary conversation that I found particularly interesting in which she felt that she had been harassed by other women. I asked her if she would tell me the story again, and she said that she didn't mind telling it to me, but asked that I maintain some confidentiality regarding the show title and its principal figures because they were still around and she felt no animosity toward them. I still thought the story was worth telling, so I agreed to her restrictions. I thought that it was a good example of some of the kinds of problems that women can have—even from members of their own sex.

Anyway, it was about ten years ago, just before I got my first assignment of *Sesame Street*, and these two women had sold a show to PBS that was to be *for* women, *about* women, and was to have been completely staffed by women, including the director. Well, they asked me if I would do it, and I jumped at the chance—but I never got into the control room. They fired me while we were still in pre-production. They told me that I "didn't exude enough of an aura of confidence for them." The real truth was that the women in the producer slots were uncomfortable with what they were doing, and I became a kind of sacrificial lamb to their own insecurity. They eventually hired a man as director.

Unfortunately, credibility becomes a terribly important factor in our business, whatever you are doing. The networks are filled with people whose jobs are always in jeopardy, especially in the programming and scheduling arenas, and none of them has the vaguest idea of what works and what doesn't, so they take no chances. They feed off clones of successful programs and the creativity of other people. It's a hard nut to crack without credits or credibility. To find the same set of rules operative at a petty PBS level is appalling. There should always be room for new ideas and new people, especially in public television.

Emily Squires is a very attractive woman, and when she first broke into the business, she must have caused a stir in the control room. I wondered, and asked, if she had ever been the victim of sexual harassment in the all-male bastion of television.

When I first became an A.D., the guys were on my case all of the time. I would wear headsets, and they would wait until they knew that I had the headset on, and then they would begin to tell the foulest jokes that you could imagine. I was such a novice at all of this, working in the control room, that they must have sensed my vulnerability. I was so protected as a production assistant and as a secretary that I had never been party to any of this before. But now I was a sitting duck, and they all were taking advantage of it, telling all these jokes, making the foulest of remarks to each other so that I would overhear them. They just went out of their way to make it as uncomfortable for me as possible.

They thought they were funny, but I think the underlying thing was that somehow or other I might be compromising their masculinity, their machoness, their male superiority. They were telling me in no uncertain way, "I don't want to take directions from a woman," and they were waiting for me to mess up, looking for anything that I might do wrong. But slowly, when I sort of proved myself, they stopped. Once you show that you are there to do a job, and that nothing they say is going to stop you from doing it, they stop, but I can't understand why women have to go through that kind of hazing. I know that it happens to women who join the police force and the fire department, but I can't conceive of it happening to a young lawyer joining a law firm or a young doctor entering the staff of a hospital. It's a crazy society.

I wanted to return to her activities on *Sesame Street* and get more detail about that, so I asked her about her schedule and how often she did the show.

At least once a week, sometimes twice a week. The show is not in production year-round. We start producing in September and usually finish around the end of January. During that period, we do ten shows a week, usually at a rate of two a day, except when we use the Muppets, and then it's a whole other ball game. We tape when they've available—which isn't often because of their busy schedule. But when they say they are available, we try and do as much as we can, get a whole backlog of Muppet inserts, which we then put in our tape library. The pieces that we do on the "street" then become the spine of the show, and when that spine is completed, then we go back to the Muppet inserts that we have stockpiled and spot them throughout the show.

As I said, I am one of several directors who do all this. For example, our producer, Lisa Simon, is also a director, which is very helpful, having another director in the control room. I love it when I hear from Lisa. She's much more than a director. Working as the producer, too, she knows all the editorial stuff, the meat of things, and that can be most helpful. In fact, I love when the writers are there. I love it when I hear from the actors. I think you can use all the help you can get, and if you have the kind of mind that closes you off from any advice or suggestions from the outside, then you shouldn't be a director.

You have to run the show—there's no question about that. But you can really use any and all input, depending on the source. Some of the actors have been in their parts for twenty years, so you know that they can help you tremendously with their characters. And the writers wrote it—that's the heart of the whole thing. A good show is usually a collaborative effort, and obviously you don't have to take every suggestion, or use them—but I hear everyone out.

On the last day that I visited Emily Squires in her *Sesame Street* control room, things seemed to be going very smoothly in spite of the fact that both Emily and Big Bird had a bad cold. The script called for the huge Henson puppet to be sick on that day, but Emily really was suffering, and still working. (I think I heard someone once say that "The show must go on!" but I never have been able to figure out why.) She had a terrible case of laryngitis, among other things, and the crew had rigged a portable mike and speaker for her, so that she could communicate with everyone on the floor while she was blocking, turning it off and on at her pleasure. It reminded me a bit of the little microphones that National Football League referees wear so they can broadcast. I asked her if she was getting special treatment, being "coddled," because she was a woman.

For goodness sakes, no! It's just that they had to hear me, so they put that mike on me. I never want to work without it; I loved that microphone. It was just great. You'd switch it off when you were talking to the cast, but when you needed something, you'd just switch the little microphone on, and say "Props," and everyone would descend on you because my voice would be broadcast over every studio speaker in the place. It was hysterical, and really quite wonderful, and yes, they would do that for a man, too. The object was to use the system sparingly, so that it really worked.

Everything on *Sesame Street* seemed to me to be geared to a child's point of view. I perceived that there was a lot of talking to camera that really didn't need to be there.

I'm not sure if that's really so. For one thing, I usually reject that as a suggestion in the script. When the script calls for "the actor talks to camera," I switch it; I change it. It's a matter of personal taste. Furthermore, it's not actually a mandate of the Children's Television Workshop, or of *Sesame Street,* that we necessarily need to communicate with the kids at home through the camera.

The other thing—when you said that the show seemed geared to kids— it's true it is a children's show, but I believe there's a certain universal standard when it comes to entertainment, and I think the Muppets have proved that better than anyone. And we've discovered that adults who watch the show like it just as much as the kids do. For one thing, *Sesame Street* doesn't talk down to the kids, and it's genuinely funny. Children are surprisingly sophisticated in their sense of humor. I mean they really pick up the jokes; nothing goes by them. You can't just let something go by carelessly; you can't just say, "Oh, this is a kid's show. No one will get this. We'll just let it pass."

I asked Emily if there were any other problems with content, things on the show that might scare an audience, for example.

The major problems, if there are any, like whether a character might scare a child, are definitely taken care of before the show gets into the studio. There were times, when we first started with the Muppet monsters, when the furor from our own research department and the mothers at home was really something. We kept getting letters: "Our kids are scared to death!" Well, I'm just not sure that fictional characters are capable of doing that, if the past can tell us anything. Long before television ever existed, writers enjoyed playing with the imagination of children. When you look through Grimm's Fairy Tales, Aesop's Fables, Hansel and Gretel, you will find that they are filled with wild imaginary creatures, and generations of kids grew up loving them. And today, there are contemporary artists and picture makers, like Maurice Sendak with his *Where the Wild Things Are* and Steven Spielberg with his *E.T.* These are quality images, so kids are stimulated by them. Children love things like that—and our Muppet monsters.

The show that I viewed that day must have been a typical "street" segment—what Emily had described as the "spine of the show." Comparing that taping to the typical *Sesame Street* "hours" that I watched during this period, I was very aware of the great amount of pre-production and post-production that must go into each episode of the show. I asked Emily how much of each show was studio based and how much rolled in during post-production.

I would say that we do about twenty or twenty-five minutes of each show in the studio—what we call the "street pieces." As I told you before, during the course of a season, when they are available, we will do certain Muppet inserts and other material, but after twenty years in production, we have a huge library of live action films, animated bits, cast inserts, Muppet inserts, none of which have aged, all of which we still use occasionally in one show or another. We have it all computerized, so that we can program the various pieces, rotate them, use them again and again, without repeating ourselves. But the "street pieces" are always new.

When we first started, we used to do an occasional complete show. As a production assistant, I had to time every tiny little segment and make sure that it all came out at 59:20, every show. But, of course, we don't have to do that now. Our final assemblage and responsibility for timing is up in editing, in the hands of a guy named Bob Emerick, who's the head of our editing group.

Once we are through with our "street" pieces, basically, the show is all done. We do very few extra bits and pieces now, we have such a huge stockpile of material, although I did do a remote this year with the Snuffleupagus, which is this huge animal with two puppeteers in it—you know, a head and a tail. Then there was the Mama Snuffleupagus, a second huge animal with a person in the head and one in the tail, and finally, there was "Baby Alice" Snuffleupagus, which only had one female puppeteer in it.

But if you can imagine the scene—on location in Central Park—the hottest day of the year, the temperature was well over a hundred degrees. It was during that really horrible hot spell that we had last summer [1988]— and here we are, with two guys in one suit, two guys in another, and a young woman in the third. The logistics of just communicating with those huge puppets were astronomical, and some of the action that we had planned was most difficult, especially on location. The main problem was that we couldn't hear them, and they couldn't hear us, and we had to solve those logistical problems first. The puppeteers have to able to see, and they have to be able to talk—not only in the immediate vicinity, but for the much larger picture that we are trying to get.

I recalled that when I was in the studio, I had seen Big Bird with his upper body removed. I noticed that he had a wireless mike, and I thought I saw a small TV set on a rig around his neck. I asked Emily if this was the usual kind of thing the puppeteers wore under their costumes.

Most of the big puppets do, and as you saw, they have these little tiny television sets rigged on their chests. Those sets were originally designed for Big Bird. He always wears that pack under his costume, and it includes a tiny microphone and a small television monitor. That rig, designed by Walt Raufer, who was our video engineer, has become the standard SONY television set that everyone sells, but we were the first to do that.

Now, what that allows, obviously, is for someone like the puppeteer in Big Bird or the Snuffleupagus, who is basically working blind, to be able to see where they are going and to be able to communicate with the control room. They can actually see the shot that we are taking. They can see the intercuts, so that they know when we are on a tight shot, or that we have gone wide, and they can act accordingly. That kind of communicating is essential to what we do.

We directed all that from a remote truck in the park and created our little drama with the Snuffleupaguses. It was really complicated, trying to be able to hear them from a great way off, and for them to be able to hear me, get a decent mix on it all and still be in contact with the cameras. It was a little bit of a nightmare as far as logistics were concerned.

I queried Emily as to whether they had two-way communication with the puppets at all times. I wondered if they could talk to the puppets at any time, while they were on the air, for example, while they were taping.

No, we can't do that, but we are in constant contact between takes, and as I said, they do see themselves on their monitors. But we finally got what we wanted, and no one died of the heat. When we came back to the studio, I edited those tapes—that's an option you can have as a director on the show, you can choose to edit your pieces. Well, they cut together like a charm, and then we did a sound mix, and it all worked out beautifully.

One of the things that surprised me in my studio visits was the height of all the sets, and then it hit me that they were dealing most of the time with oversized characters like Big Bird and the Snuffleupagus. I asked Emily if there were any shooting problems when you equate large puppets with normal-sized human beings—or vice versa, small puppets with people.

Humongus! I don't know if this was happening on the day that you were there or not, but those discrepancies are constantly hitting us between the eyes. I wonder when we're ever going to learn. Something like Snuffy is so huge, and then, in the same shot, you are trying to get some of these other puppets that are really tiny. Like we had a cow—a cow puppet, right—and we had a Snuffleupagus. Well, a normal-size cow puppet is relatively small when you compare it to a human body, but when it's in a shot with one of the cast members, somehow or other the size difference doesn't really matter. It's when you get that cow with a big thing like the Snuffleupagus that your eye just refuses to accept the size difference; putting the two in the same shot just points up the fact that the cow is a puppet—exactly what you *don't* want.

So we have those kind of spatial problems all of the time, and height problems, and seeing puppeteers' heads, and trying to figure out where you are going to place the body of your puppeteer so that he can appear at the same height level as a member of the cast. Puppets play one on one with humans all of the time on the show, so we create all kinds of little places within the set where we have slots and holes and areas for the puppets—places the puppeteers can hide behind and position their puppet, put little feet on it, so it looks like he's just sitting there.

All of this was worked out a long time ago by Jim Henson and Frank Oz. They're not around as much as they used to be, but the young puppeteers who have replaced them have all been trained by Henson and work pretty much the way that he did.

When you work with Jim, you know what he likes and what he doesn't. Your ego suffers when you work with Jim because he doesn't rave about things. You just know when he likes something and when he doesn't.

Best of all, he's funny. He knows how to make things work on camera, how to make situations pay off. When you see Frank Oz and Jim working together, it's just heaven to watch. They make the most mundane things and situations hysterically funny—nothing defeats them. And it's so great how he has made all of this pay off for them so well. Frank Oz has become a major picture director, the Muppets are a major producing entity and Miss Piggy has become a big star. I don't know what we would do if we lost Frank or Jim. Frank Oz *is* the Cookie Monster; Jim Henson *is* Kermit the Frog. There's no replacing *them*. Then, too, Frank plays Bert to Jim's Ernie, and he plays Grover—I mean, I could go on and on. How do you replace people like that?

Now that Jim Henson has become so successful, I asked Emily if she felt that *Sesame Street* was still getting the best examples of Jim's work—what Miss Piggy describes as the "crème de la crème"—or was that all going into Henson's movies or his own TV programs and specials?

Well, it certainly isn't a case of not doing his best every time he is committed to a project, because, of course, he does; he would never do anything which isn't absolutely perfect, as far as he's concerned. But he obviously has more time and more money when he's working on his own features and specials to do more elaborate technical setups and that sort of thing.

Like Kermit riding on his bicycle in the first Muppet movie. Do you remember that? It was unbelievable how they managed it. It was all done by remote control. There Kermit was, in a wide shot, riding his bicycle down a road; his mouth moved, he was singing a song and his feet were working the pedals on the bike. In fact, I think that Kermit's whole body moved, or at least, I believe that it did, which is part of Jim's artistry. He does that kind of thing all of the time now. The possibilities are endless with him, and we are fortunate that we still see a lot of his work on our show.

I wondered if there were any kinds of specific directorial problems that Emily faced when dealing with the Muppets and working with Jim Henson.

I don't know if you are familiar with the kinds of sets that we use when we are doing Muppet inserts. The sets are always built way above the heads of the puppeteers so that they can stand with their arms straight up over their heads and work the puppets that way. Now there are times that they work seated, but most of the time they work standing up, and Jim is about 6 feet, 2 inches tall, so that alone can be sort of distancing.

"How do you cover them?" I asked. "Do you work off of a crane or a dolly?"

No, we just keep the camera on high ped most of the time, and that usually covers it.

And that's pretty much what I do when we are shooting the Muppets. I just lay back and watch them work because it's only when the puppeteers get together and start interacting with each other that the bits really come alive. My cameras are just reporting, so basically, as a director, about the only thing you can do is let them go, let them do their thing. Provide the situation, provide the basic physical moves and the blocking that will allow their creativity free rein and then let them go and work out amongst themselves the things that are really needed to make a piece sing—to go from just being a bit to something that's a hysterically funny Muppet bit.

It's very difficult to move on those Muppet sets anyway; they're so small and basically so flat. There's very little depth and limited head room, so the angles are very critical, very minimal. Worst of all, you can't go for too many singles; the puppets are too small, and cross shooting is differ-ent—and even that is not at the kind of angles that you would get on a set where there is a lot more depth. It's a very specific kind of shooting, videotaping the Muppets—totally different from the shooting that we do on the set with the "street" material.

There wasn't much more that needed to be said. About the only thing more I wanted to get from Emily was the story of her involvement with an organization called New York Women in Film. She is a member of their board of directors, and I was interested in hearing what the group was and what their goals were.

Well, it's a group of about three hundred women, and they really are extraordinary. I don't belong to many organizations, but this one is really special—the women, what they do—there are vice-presidents of major film companies, a lot of fine documentary film makers, a great many producers of film and television programs. It's a meeting place for these women who get together once a month to learn from each other, from guest speakers, special programs and seminars.

My role on the board is to act as a kind of liaison between the organization and a new workshop that we're putting together for women directors. We're planning this in conjunction with the American Film Institute in Los Angeles, and we will be using the facilities of the School of Visual Arts here in New York. There's nothing like it here on the East Coast that's exclusively for women. You asked me earlier how we were going to get more women into the director's chair, and I think this is one way to do it. I'm very excited about all this, and my participation in it.

Eventually our hope is to subsidize chosen candidates, give them a certain amount of money, enough to make a short film. Our primary thrust is going to be in film, but oddly enough, everyone is going to be working on videotape, primarily because of the exigencies of time and money. We're going to choose five women in our first group, and we'll put them through a series of seminars, everything from soup to nuts: audio engineering, lighting, how to deal with actors, how to block a show, how to conduct a rehearsal, how to use their time creatively—we'll try and cover everything. In addition, every candidate will be working with a mentor of some note, probably a major film director—someone like Susan Seidelman, who's on our board, or Robert Benton, Elaine May, Barry Levinson, or Penny Marshall. Hopefully, by the end of this course, they will have written a script and shot a major piece of videotape or film. The final product will air first on the Lifetime Cable channel.

I think a workshop like this can be genuinely helpful in motivating people, getting them started if they show the talent on a career in television or film direction. The ratio of women to men in the professions has grown enormously over the past fifteen years: the law, medicine, business, almost everything except television. Maybe something like this can help change that. I think women need to be more secure in themselves, know that they have something to say, know that they are just as capable of saying it as men.

I asked Emily Squires one last question: How much had she been able to write over the years, and had that helped her as a director?

I have written several soaps over the years. I was one of the writers on *Search for Tomorrow*, and I wrote *Guiding Light* for a while, and *As the World Turns*. I've written several screenplays, too, only one of which has ever been sold, but I doubt if it will ever see the inside of a movie theatre. But writing has really helped me as a director. It has given me a great sense of security with the scripts I get in the studio and has been really helpful when it comes to working with actors, understanding their motivation, being able to guide them through the nuances of a story.

I plan to continue my writing, but even more I would like to write *and* direct my own script. I know that there are major dangers in that. Even if you get a good strong producer to work with, it's still sort of myopic— but something I'd love to try. I've come close a couple of times on scripts that I've written, and who knows, one these days I may be able to pull it off. Wouldn't that be wonderful? You'll see my credit on the screen: written, produced, and directed by Emily Squires.

☆ **10**

George Paul: Directing *Today*

George Paul works in a pressure cooker. His job reminds me of the summer job that I once had working for the Carnegie-Illinois Steel Company in South Chicago, Indiana. I was a laborer during my college summers, employed as a "gandy dancer" on the narrow gauge railroad which joined the various sections of the large mill, and I was particularly fascinated by the men who worked in and around the blast furnaces, surrounded by molten metal. To me, it seemed that these men were always in constant danger: a few drops of rain water in the bottom of a mold into which hot steel was being poured could cause the whole thing to blow out, spewing the liquid steel around their working area. When we were doing work in and around the blast furnaces, our narrow gauge crew got in and out of there in a hell of a hurry. And, of course, all the men working there loved it; they relished the danger of the job and just wouldn't think of working any place else.

I'm not sure if the analogy holds completely, comparing a job in "live" television with the vicissitudes of working with hot steel. Do we toy with life and death in the work place every time that we step into a control room to the extent that it happens in a steel mill? Well, maybe that's a little much, but I'm sure that the emotional and physical toll of what George Paul does must be great. And knowing him, I am even more positive that he ignores his physician's constant admonitions to "take it easy." For, like the steel workers, George likes what he does, directing the *Today* show, every day, live, on the NBC network, for two hours.

It was difficult to get George to agree to an interview. First of all, I don't think he sits still for anybody—certainly not someone not directly connected to his show. Then, too, we were in contact

George Paul (© 1989 National Broadcasting Company, Inc.)

during the intensely political summer and fall of 1988, when George not only was doing the *Today* show but also was involved in covering the political conventions of both parties for NBC; traveling to Seoul, South Korea, to cover the Olympics; doing NBC's election night coverage; and from my perception, working on almost anything and everything that the network broadcast from the day of my first conversation with him until he finally invited me to join him in the *Today* control room.

It seemed almost anticlimactic to finally sit with him after the show in his office on the third floor at 30 Rockefeller Plaza in New York, the home of the National Broadcasting Company, and talk to him about how all of this began:

I started in television in 1952 with WBKB-TV, the ABC-owned and -operated television station in Chicago, as an assistant auditor, and from that, I moved up to become radio program business manager for WLS, the Prairie Farmer station in Chicago, another ABC-owned property. Titles were handed out in those days—lots of titles, and little or no money.

Not long after that, in 1953, ABC merged with Paramount Theatres, and a new regime came in; a new controller of the company was appointed. Well, the new people said that I could stay on, but to forget the fancy title; I'd now be an accountant.

"Do you like the job, Mr. Paul?" I was asked. "Absolutely," I replied. So I became an accountant and was that for about a year, and I kept seeing all these people around with smiles on their faces, and I thought I might like to find out what *they* did, and I was told that they were in something called "production."

It was then that I decided to become a stage manager. In those days, they were called floor managers. We got fancy, I think, along about 1960. But I was given that opportunity in 1954, and three years later, in 1957, I became a staff television director at WBKB-TV in Chicago, which is about 31 years ago. That's a long time ago.

I told George that of all the directors I had ever interviewed or talked to, his was the strangest career route I have ever heard of anyone taking—going from accountant to director. I asked if he ever had any idea that he was going to go this way, if he had any notions about show business as he was growing up.

Not too much. I had been in some plays as a young person. I think my first was *Our Town*. I played Cy Crowell, who was kept busy on the stage selling an imaginary paper or two in Grover's Corners, New Hampshire. That was in high school.

And I was in *George Washington Slept Here,* which was done in a community theatre. Then, one time, I was with a touring company of *Kiss and Tell,* which had been playing in Chicago. I replaced the kid doing the part, who had an appendicitis attack, so I did that show for six weeks. It was 1944, right in the middle of World War II. As a result, I got my Actor's Equity card, and I made $175 a week, and you know, at that time, that was big money, especially for a young guy.

I couldn't quite understand the theatrical involvement, coming as it did out of left field. I wondered if George felt that he had any special inclination toward the theatre, toward eventually becoming a director, perhaps, and if he had any theatrical training to support the wish.

The only training that I had was two years of accountancy in night school, which doesn't sound like it makes too much sense for a guy who was going to spend his life working in television, but I'm glad that I had it, that I was in the business end for a time, because after that I always knew, almost instinctively, what the cost of things was, and what to pursue and what not to pursue—from a budgetary standpoint—as a director in television.

That training did me more good than any schooling I might have had training me for the theatre or teaching me about television. Besides, when I started, there was no way you could read about television; the books hadn't been written yet. I learned on the job, back in the days of live television. There's very little of that around now.

I asked George about his beginnings in Chicago television and what some of his first assignments in "production" were.

For one thing, I was stage manager on *Super Circus.* That was a program broadcast each week with Claude Kirchner as the Ring Master and with Mary Hartline in a tight drum majorette's outfit leading the band. I worked in the circus pit, which meant that I would jump up and down every time a performer would give a brilliant performance and plead for applause. As they finished, each performer would hold one hand up high in the air— what they called in the circus a "style"—and that would be my signal to leap onto the floor of the pit and wave at this group of kids in our audience. If I just motioned toward them, they went crazy, making lots of noise, applauding until their hands hurt. It was wonderful stuff, television, back in those days. Not too many people knew how it was done, but it was exciting, really exciting.

The first thing that I ever directed by myself was a series of five-minute spots for a news, weather, and sports show, which was broadcast from 11 to 11:30 P.M. each evening, and I got used to things happening rather quickly. There weren't a lot of films to roll in those days. Most of what we did were AP stills, which were pasted on cards and placed on music stands, which sometimes wiggled and sometimes didn't. And the weather maps didn't resemble all that fancy gadgetry that we have today. We just had a guy stand in front of a map that was kind of marked up—kind of.

After a couple of years, I produced and directed a program called *Polka Go Round*, which was broadcast live out of Chicago on the ABC television network for over two years. That was a great experience working in Chicago. I wish that I had started in production maybe five years earlier than I did. By the time I began, many of the people who had pioneered all those great early shows had moved on; I was really in the last days of network affiliate television. There weren't too many programs left; they were starting to become like dinosaurs—extinct.

And most of those great people who had done those shows were moving on. The bright and shining stars were going east and west, to New York and Hollywood—people like Bill Hoban, Bob Banner and Dave Garroway.

By the 1960s Chicago was virtually deserted as a network production center. Almost 95 percent of the production that was being done—the sitcoms, the hour shows—was being done from Hollywood, which was also a vigorous and lively production center for local programming with seven stations competing aggressively for audiences in the market. George joined the staff of one of the biggest and the best of those stations, KNBC, the NBC-owned and -operated station in Los Angeles. It was 1969.

I was a staff director out there for seven years, did a multitude of all kinds of programs: news, sports, studio productions of all kinds. Nancy Wilson had a ninety-minute variety show; Cannonball Adderly also had a show for a while, featuring his music and some talk; Billy Eckstein had a jazz show. It was great working with all of those people.

I also did a documentary with Jack Lemmon, which took me to Europe for the first time. The show was about pollution worldwide.

I was with KNBC for seven years, from 1969 to 1976. During that time I worked with such people as Tom Snyder, Tom Brokaw, Bryant Gumbel, and Steve Friedman, who became the executive producer of the *Today* show. Every one of those people ended up in New York, which by then was the production center for news and public affairs.

But I was just starting a program with Tom Snyder in Hollywood called *Sunday*, which was going to be a community affairs show in Tom's unique style, going to different locations in the Los Angeles area, talking about the things that might affect those particular areas, with all kinds of people on camera. The show was on for a couple of years, but Tom finally left, moved on to New York to do the *Tomorrow* show, which started in 1974.

Two years after Tom made his move, I got him to come back to L.A. for a fifth-anniversary special that we were doing on the *Sunday* show, which I was still directing for KNBC. That weekend Tom told me that he wanted me to come to New York to direct the *Tomorrow* show. He said, "It's a crazy life, but I need you."

So I moved and started doing the *Tomorrow* show. That was 1976, and I directed the last six years of the show. For most of that time, it was done in New York, but then we went back to the West Coast again for what at the time was called *Tomorrow Coast to Coast*. That was an idea of Freddie Silverman's, who was then the head of programming at NBC. We had Rona Barrett, the gossip columnist on the program for approximately three weeks, and when she left, the title stayed, and we lasted for about a year. That was the eighth and final year—the end of the *Tomorrow* show.

Coming back to the East Coast again, with Tom, to do a show called *Prime Time Sunday*, I wasn't sure where I was by that time. *Prime Time Sunday* was another unsuccessful effort by NBC to enter the program market with something like *60 Minutes*. I'm not sure what number try that was, but we've never been able to do it yet. But we had *Prime Time Sunday, Prime Time Saturday, Prime Time Friday,* and we still didn't find the formula. When Tom eventually left the show, I started working with David Brinkley, and that was called *NBC Magazine with David Brinkley*; I also did *NBC Magazine* without David Brinkley. And when that was cancelled, Steve Friedman, who was by then the executive producer of *Today*, offered me the job as the principal director on *Today*, which was in 1980.

George had once told me that he had seen a lot of changes on *Today* in those eight years. I asked him now what some of those changes were.

From what it was when I started? Well, it used to be a show with long, drawn out segments before Steve Friedman became the executive producer. Since he took over, and this is also true of Marty Ryan, who is now the executive producer, the pace of the show has quickened. Steve and Marty are both people who believe in lots of things happening. You see more extensive use of graphics. There are a lot more remotes on the show, so there's a lot of live involvement—feeds from all over, people talking to Jane and Bryant. But even there, it's always something where no one guest is on the program for too long. So, as I said, compared to what it was when I started, the pace has increased a great deal. We do a lot of things very quickly.

Some of the things that I've changed? When I first started on the show, the entire set was painted blue and covered with fake flowers. The whole thing looked like an ice palace; it was a very, very cold look. The desk was even blue. I thought it made all the people look blue. So I had the set repainted and toned down on some of that blue. It improved things immeasurably, immediately.

Then I decided to kill the blowups. When I started on the show, we'd have a blowup for each of the segments. A guest would come up with some subject—say he was promoting a book—we'd immediately make a large blowup of that book, and it would sit between Jane or Bryant and the guest. I got rid of that kind of look. I thought it made us look like *The Merv Griffin Show.*

For another thing, there's never been an audience on *Today,* but the chairs used to be faced outward, more or less as if the cast were playing to an audience. I changed that so that people would be sitting facing toward one another, which I thought would invite a warmer feeling of conversation, rather than looking for a response from a studio audience that wasn't out there.

Then I decided that the show needed a place where everyone got together, as opposed to everything being in limbo, abstract—some kind of cameo setting. I saw nothing wrong in having a room of some sort, a living room that wasn't copied after *Good Morning America,* and so we changed the whole set around. You've got to remember, in those days, for whatever reason, we were not leading in the ratings, so it was fairly easy for me to convince Steve that was what we should do.

Since that time there's always been one area where there is a desk, which we refer to as home base. The desk sits in front of a large panoramic photo of Manhattan, of somewhere like just opposite 30 Rock, looking east. Our second area is more or less like a living room; there are comfortable chairs and a sofa where we usually do our interviews in the studio, and it invites a little different feeling for conversation. It's a place where people can sit more comfortably than the way they used to, with some blowup staring you in the face.

Some of the things that George Paul told me about seemed relatively insignificant in the retelling, but the more I thought about them, the more I began to believe how truly insightful he was in making those changes. If you expect an audience to view your daily machinations, they have to feel a sense of comfort in the actions and reactions of your performers, and a confused set can be the first element in destroying that ease in viewing. Who was the Broadway critic who reviewed one labored musical by saying "The audience went out singing the set!" I think in most cases we do too much. I try to remember the Bauhaus admonition that "Less is More" when I prepare a setting for anything that I do in television.

Like so many other fine directors, George was scrupulous in his attention to detail, so I wanted to know exactly what his day consisted of, what his routine was, what he checked when he came into the studio as early as he did, what he could rehearse at that time of the morning.

On the day before the show, the night crew sets the scenery in place for the following day's program, and that all has to be checked out. We have a very small studio, and we work under a different set of circumstances at 30 Rockefeller Plaza as opposed to other programs which might be done in Burbank, for instance, where you have just one studio crew handling the setup of a show. Here in New York, there's a dress crew that works in the daytime, a night crew that works only at night, and a studio crew that works the show. So that was something I had to get used to doing— checking all that activity by three different crews.

The way the program has now developed is that we are going full blast as early as 4:30 in the morning, when we prepare many of the bumpers with network graphics that go into our program each day. There are visuals which have to be shot, different ones every day. There are different effects every day. Most of what we do changes from day to day, and all of this has to be supervised.

And, as you know, the program goes on at seven o'clock every morning, Monday through Friday, and it's not completely spontaneous; there are things which have to be rehearsed, like music, for example. The big question is always whether you rehearse your music prior to the show or following the show. But I believe it's best to get those things out of the way before your show; that way it usually doesn't take as much time as it does if you are rehearsing an act for the following day. So we have very early calls for musicians who are called in to rehearse for us.

It's a difficult thing to have to say to people, "You have to come in at such-and-such a time. We want to start rehearsing at 5:30 in the morning." Most musicians haven't gone to bed by that time, let alone get up and rehearse. We get to hear a lot more groans than we hear "Okay, we'll be there." The interesting point of all that is that here's this opportunity to be seen by a great number of people, and one night's sleep shouldn't make that much difference. Our objective is to make the "bit" both look good and sound good, and you just can't do that without rehearsal. The performer should also be able to put a little into the pot, but that's always a sticky situation. Sometimes they just don't want to show up for rehearsal, even though they are going to perform. I must say that I don't like it, but I have done things under all kinds of circumstances. If a person doesn't want to come in early and rehearse, we'll go ahead and do the spot anyway.

I remember one time last year we did a last-minute booking of the entire cast of *Ain't Misbehavin'*. Well, you know you just can't take the cast of a Broadway show and put them on camera without rehearsal, shoot it off the cuff. Well, luckily, the producers and the performers knew that as well as we did, and they were protecting their investment in the show. They wanted everything to look spectacular, so they brought the entire cast in early. We were able to run it through a couple of times, and the spot looked just great.

I've seen all kinds of performers. They run the whole gamut, from cooperative to—what shall I say?—as if they are doing us a favor. If anybody's doing anyone a favor, we're doing it for them. They can't buy the kind of publicity that they get on our show, and we see 'em going up the ladder, as well as going down.

I know that time of the morning's a hell of a time to rehearse, but we have the people waiting for them, and they're wide awake. The crew is always there on time; they're a special breed of people who like to work those kind of hours, and we treat them accordingly. I don't ever feel that a crew should be overrehearsed anyway, ever.

Besides, I'm someone who likes to direct under calculated chaos, a little bit short of pandemonium, and although I know how crucial additional run-throughs can be, especially in a performance that's finer edged, and I like that—I'd rather hear someone ask for "one more run-through" than hear someone say, "Jesus, do we have to rehearse this again?"—I can go either way. I have people regularly assigned to the program, and they know what they have to do, blindfolded.

Whatever we do, we generally try and look at things a little bit differently, and I hope we are successful at it. I guess we are, if the ratings are any indication. I try not to look at them, nor have I ever really watched what the opposition is doing. Only on occasion, when somebody on the back deck over there, the "journalists" of our program, want me to check something out, will I look at something. I feel very strongly that we have to do our own thing.

I must admit that I was a bit overwhelmed on the day that I sat in the *Today* control room for two hours and watched George do his thing. It's a big control room, almost as large as the studio that the show comes from. By air time, it's packed, too, with everyone from the executive producer, Marty Ryan, down to a couple of production assistants, busy making the myriad number of "on-the-air" changes that a show like *Today* is prone to.

But the thing that impressed me the most was the overwhelming number of functioning, operating monitors in the control room. Each, with a different picture on it, was designated with a small sign indicating its point of origin, and in most cases, supervisory personnel were already in touch with the faces on those monitors, even though it was well before air time, checking on the details of who, what, why, or when for the segments that would be fed into the show later in the morning. I asked George if he would give me an equipment breakdown on the show: Exactly how many monitors, for example, were there in the *Today* control room, and did he find that at all confusing?

Studio 3-B, where we broadcast from every day, has probably the largest control room of any of the network's facilities. We have approximately seventy monitors in that room. I feel most comfortable when there are more of them on than less. In fact, I even enjoy it when we have the talent coming in and actually sitting in there, working the show from the control room.

I might note that NBC has one of its new robotic cameras mounted in the corner of the *Today* control room. George rarely uses it, except for an occasional bumper or cutaway, but taking him at his word, I assume that he has also "worked the show" from there.

I mean that's my Yankee Stadium. I've often wondered about the cockpits of airplanes—if a pilot really looks at all the dials in front of him. On the big planes, there are other guys in there; somebody's got to be looking at all those other dials that he's not seeing. To some stranger sitting up there, I could see that it might look overwhelming. And the same is true in 3-B. It only looks imposing; it's not to me; it's very comfortable.

On first impression, it might look complex, but what it really narrows down to is a two-camera shoot. When I'm dealing with Jane and Bryant, it's just a matter of putting the camera where it should be, not too soon, and certainly not too late. You have to be there, no matter how many cameras you are using. I have four studio cameras, and one in the control room that's unmanned, but with those four cameras I can do almost anything I want to do in the studio. With most of the interviews, I only require two cameras. I don't put a camera in the center to see if the guest and the interviewer are facing each other. I don't believe in that.

I have shot the *Today* show, ever since I started, from over the shoulder. That's probably the same kind of technique that I used when I was on the *Tomorrow* show. So you only need two cameras for that—one over each of the people's shoulders into the face of the other. That center two-shot always seems to me to be saying, "Ta-dah! There they are!" And I find that superfluous, unnecessary. When a person's intense, I want that camera up close, looking right in his face, closer than most people go with a camera. A person is gesticulating, using his hands; it's my responsibility to show that movement. But I think the day of the center two-shot is really over, a thing of the past.

In the old days, it used to be a standard thing. Three cameras: one on each side, one in the center. There used to be turrets with lenses on them on the front of the cameras, and you'd have to call up a specific lens. To me, that was a lot more challenging; you really had to plan your shots. Now, with these zoom lenses, all you have to say to your cameras is "tighten the shot a little bit. A little tighter, a little tighter, a little tighter," and that's it. It doesn't take too much brains to do that, as opposed to really knowing what it was all about: "Give me a 135, give me a 90, give me an 8½." Or a 50 mm, which was the widest lens of all. But now the jargon of the television director has narrowed down to one sentence, "Tighten the shot a bit, that's fine, hold it there"—as opposed to calling up the proper lens, calculating the distance between the cameras and the subject, which as you know, also affects the focal length between your people, or whatever you were shooting.

Zoom lenses have made the job a lot easier—there's no doubt about that—but I don't think it's as challenging as it was. I remember days when we'd do shows that I would say to the camera operators, "Camera One has two shots with a 50, then you go to a 90, and then to a 135. There are four shots in all." "Camera Two has a 135, and an 8½, and a 90." Camera Three had another completely different assortment of lenses. And the camera operators would write those things down or memorize them, and the lenses would flip, and it would all work like a charm. Now it's a brainless process; the cameramen don't have to memorize anything. I just say, "Tighten that shot up a little bit, or loosen it," and that's it. It's a different world.

To me, the complexity of *Today* came from what George Paul managed in his control room. NBC is electronically and digitally in the vanguard, which is what you would expect from one of the three major networks. But sitting in the control room, seeing it all in operation was something else again. The magnitude of it was mind-boggling. Open lines to affiliates, satellite feeds from around the world, and all that technology that just didn't exist nine or ten years ago: squeeze zooms, blowouts, electronic wipes. It looked like the War Room at the Pentagon in the midst of a nuclear counteroffensive. The changes were startling, even for someone like myself who had spent a great portion of his working life in control rooms.

I can remember seeing an early version of the *Today* show long ago, viewing it from my bedroom as I was preparing to go to work. Dave Garroway was doing it, and the Russians had just put the first manned Sputnik up in space, and Dave was trying to talk to a visiting Russian scientist who was a guest lecturer at the Massachusetts Institute of Technology in Boston. No picture—they were just trying to get a two-way telephone line, a PL, to the NBC affiliate up there. They were having little or no success, and Dave swore. It was the first time I had ever heard anyone on television use profanity, and he did it in anger: "Goddammit! The Russians have got a man up in space, and we can't even make a phone call to Boston!"

I told George how surprised I was to see these things, the feeds and such, being done with such relative ease and such facility. It struck me as a terribly difficult and responsible job: the cueing that he did, the extent of the connections that were at his finger tips; he could communicate with almost any place in the world. I thought of it as a tremendous responsibility; the complexity of his roll-ins and satellite feeds made for an enormous burden on the part of the director. I asked how he coped with all of that.

Well, it is something, as you tell it, but then you must remember that it's become almost second nature to me—the flow of the show, where my eyes have to look, when to take something and when not to take it. I am also helped out by a back deck of people who are involved with every step of what I do in the control room. They set up the feeds, see that the guest is there and knows what he has to say, or is supposed to say. If the feed is not any good, and there are all kinds of problems—things that can go wrong with overseas remotes—they stay with it until it's right, and that can sometimes continue until a few seconds before we take that feed. The taking of those shots is my responsibility, and I don't get too concerned about whether the feed is a good one or not. I just assume that it's all going to work; obviously, I wouldn't have that confidence without that big support system. The taking of those feeds has become second nature to me. I don't even think about them. It's just something that I do, that I react to every day, and the more there are, the better. In fact, when there aren't a multiple amount of challenges like that, it's kind of a boring day.

I asked George to tell me what a typical day on the show would consist of.

Today we had a pre-tape with Frankfurt and a second one with Moscow because of the Armenian earthquake. We rarely tape anything before 6:00 or 6:30 in the morning, but because there's a five- or six-hour time differential, and the piece from Frankfurt was something that was going to happen at 5:15, our time, we opened up a little early.

Almost immediately following that, there was a pre-tape from Moscow at 6:00, and there was no communication with Moscow Control. The communication just dropped out, so I wound up talking directly to the guest in Moscow and asked him to have the camera operator tighten the shot up for us.

But the audience sees none of that—and shouldn't. They are only interested in the end result because that's all that happens for them. There's no running commentary on the screen explaining our activities. It's happening as it's happening, and that's it. If we think of ourselves as professionals, we are committed to getting our story on the screen, whatever it is. How it gets there is something else again—and should be kept one of those untold secrets. I'm not sure if the average viewer is really very interested anyway.

I wasn't sure if I completely agreed with that. In this age of media manipulation, I have the feeling that we should get our audience even more involved than they are, that we should let it all hang out if it happens that way, especially in the dispensation of the news. Maybe if they knew more about what goes on behind the camera, they wouldn't be so prone to the "sound byte" mentality that is presently plaguing our political system. It might help us to discover the whys and wherefores of the sleek, packaged messages that our politicians and presidents dole out to us. I am much more interested to find out if the people in our public offices can write a simple declarative sentence than if they can give me ten seconds of nonsense on the nightly news.

A recent successful movie, *Broadcast News,* made us party to some of that deception. One very amusing scene showed us a last-minute tape editing, with the completed version being rushed to air, with a terrific knee slide to boot. I enjoyed it thoroughly. I felt that the *Today* show had some of that same manic quality about it— something that I always felt would break loose at any moment— and only George's mastery of the scene held it together. He told me one quick story about chaos in the control room that I particularly relished—so much so that I decided to use it as the title to this collection. "I can't tell you how many times," he told me, "in the panic of the control room, I have turned to my technical director, and shouted, 'TAKE ONE!' and then have him turn to me and say, 'George, you're already on *one.*' "

We continued to talk about the great number of feeds that the show had, both live and as taped roll-ins. There are even two co-related remote positions at NBC that feed tapes for the show. I couldn't even consider the number of things that were fed into the show each day. I estimated about ten a day for the news alone— and I was way off.

More than that. In the news there are approximately six or seven per newscast, and there are four newscasts in the two-hour show, so there may be twenty-five to thirty tapes per program that we roll in. Sometimes it's more than that; we've had as many as one hundred separate tapes on a show. I mean that's quite a lot, and every one of them is as important as the next; you can't screw them up.

It's a detail business, and every detail, every facet of the show, every item that comes into the studio needs examination. Just misspell one person's name on your credits, and you'll think that someone blew up the building. And you've got to convey that to all people that you work with, that every minute that you spend preparing a routine for your next day's show is important—crucial. You want everyone that you work with to know everything that's going to happen, down to the smallest detail.

The t's have to be crossed. Some people don't think that something small like that is important. But the whole business is made up of minutiae—so much so that no matter what job a person does, they should never feel that what they do is something less than someone with a more glorified title is doing. Everything and everybody in a show like ours are important. And that's also true of every show I've ever worked.

I truly believe that, and there isn't a person who works for me who doesn't know that, from a camera operator to a cable puller. Every person is equally important, and this isn't corny. I really feel this, and I think I've always been most successful in conveying this to the peole that I work with.

The phone started to ring on George Paul's desk, and I could feel his attention wavering. There was a problem on the set that needed his good eye, and I felt our interview coming to an end. There were still so many things that I wanted to ask him, mainly about his diversity. George does many more things than the *Today* show. One of his official titles is Director of NBC's Convention and Election Coverage. I wanted to know what happened to the *Today* show when he was off doing something else.

I've been very lucky. I do a lot of great stuff for the network. I covered the 1988 summit in Moscow, the Summer Olympics in Seoul. I covered both the Republican and Democratic conventions in New Orleans and Atlanta, NBC's election night coverage with Tom Brokaw. In fact, I get called on for almost everything at the network that's a live special event.

I like to think that *Today* falls apart when I'm gone, but it doesn't. There are always capable people to take over. The show will occasionally piggyback on some of these big events, broadcasting from the location, even from the same setting as the event, but I try not to involve myself when I'm doing the big event. I think my work suffers when I'm split like that.

I want all of my attention and my concentration on the single task that I am doing; anything else can become a distraction.

I told George that he must keep his bag packed all of the time. Not only was he traveling the world doing all of these special things, but also I was aware of *Today's* touring. I knew this gave them a great boost in the ratings, and as a consequence, they, too, were always on the road. I asked him about some of the places that they had taken the show and some of the attendant problems.

Everywhere. Moscow, Rome, London, Rio, Buenos Aires, Australia, China. You name it, we've been there. Last year we took a trip on the Orient Express, stopping each morning in a different European city: Paris, Zurich, Munich, Vienna and Venice. We had our control room set up in the baggage car of the train, and every day we would beam up to the satellite and broadcast "live" at our normal air time, intercutting with the studio in New York for the news and the weather.

It was quite an operation. You couldn't do that without having extraordinary advance people readying everything for you, so that when you move into town, all that you've got to do is switch on the cameras. I don't mean to intimate that it's a piece of cake, for it can all get a little "hairy" at times.

We use a lot of local people when we are out on the road, especially if we are in the States. There are so many good people out there, good production people who are working at local stations all over this country, who for one reason or another haven't made that move to the "big city." Just because you are working locally doesn't mean that you're not good enough to be at the network. If you want to make the move, you've got to get a break—someone, somewhere who says, "You're the person who can do the job!" I spent nineteen years working in Chicago and Burbank— almost a lifetime—before my big break came.

Tom Snyder was the person who believed in me and gave me the chance of going to the network. As I told you, I directed the *Tomorrow* show with Tom for six great years, 1976 to 1982. Those were exciting days with Tom; he was a great motivator. And it was always done in one take. "Keep on going, George," he would tell me. "We don't stop for anything!" I learned that from him, and that's what's so great about *Today*, it's always done on the first take—there isn't any Take Two.

In spite of the chaotic nature of what he did, I found that George was surprisingly calm in the middle of all that pressure. In fact, I found him surprisingly funny, and the more the heat was on, the funnier he got. He reminded me of another director that I had worked with many years before at CBS by the name of Tim Kiley. Timmy was constantly "on" in the control room with an unending line of jokes and chatter, and like George, this went on while working live on the network. But Timmy was also the best prepared of any director that I had ever known; he had done his homework to such an extent that he knew every shot in the script by heart. I thought about his behavior a great deal, and it made great sense to me; this was Timmy's way of working off the tension engendered by what he did. I assume that the same is true of George Paul. I remembered his first remarks to his crew shortly before air time as he put on his phones: "Let's get along today, guys." I'd heard directors say a lot of things to crews as they go on the air, but that line was a first for me. I asked him about it.

They're a good bunch, and I need them. I need them badly, and it's awfully early in the morning. I guess it's just my way of telling them that.

I also told him that there were a lot of other things that I heard in his control room that I had never heard before—all kinds of unique phrases and directions that I was sure that no one had ever read in any instructional book on television. It took me a few minutes to figure them all out: "blow back," "box it," "sunburst," "whip out," "fishtank," "glitz," "random 39." I asked him about the visual shorthand.

I don't know. I guess it's something that I do just to keep the crew in good humor or, better still, keep them on their toes. It's a long, hard week that everyone puts in, and I guess this is just my way of telling them that they are one of the best crews around, and we are doing one of the best shows around, and besides, you all know what I'm talking about anyway.

That seemed about as good a place as any to stop, so I asked George Paul about what he sees for himself in the upcoming years.

I certainly will continue to do *Today*, for one thing, for as long as my contract continues, I'm sure. I am not going to Hollywood and make a movie; I'm quite content doing what I'm doing, where I am, working on *Today*, with the people that I work with.

And fortunately, I'm also able to do a lot of other projects, which are usually things which are a bit out of the norm. I think it's just great to be what I am, a live television director. There are very few of us left; we're becoming extinct, just like the whooping crane. Being a live television director is something I never envisioned for myself, but it's what I became, and still am—and it's the greatest.

☆

Postlude

The interviews in this book were conducted over a period of five years, between 1983 and 1988, in the production centers of Los Angeles and New York City. As I reread them, going back over what I have documented, I have a small pang of regret that I hadn't laid down more hard and fast rules at the start to elicit more comparative statements and viewpoints. What I found instead were voices with experience, directors who were willing to discuss their art and how they achieve it, but who were not dogmatic about their methodology. I have found what they had to say insightful, and I know the reader will.

Some, of course, were more articulate about the process than others. There is a certain amount of diversity in approach and technique among the people whom I talked to, but all of them were as eager to explore what they did as I was to document it. Not all agreed on how things should be done: Kirk Browning told us how heavily he counts on the close-up, continuously going tight; Larry Auerbach theorized that the day of the tight shot is over, lost in the peripheral vision of the room that we are viewing in. George Schaefer expressed a preference for videotape over film; conversely, Paul Bogart preferred film. Don Mischer stressed the importance of technical background; Marc Daniels noted his ignorance of anything mechanical.

Fortunately, continuity was present as we went from piece to piece. I asked most of the directors some of the same questions and got similar answers, but there were always individual nuances on how a particular director's art is achieved. On reflection, I don't think that these quirks in how directors do their "thing" matter that much, and certainly this does not detract from the heart of what I hope this book will convey.

What is universal among them relates more to the abstract than to dogma, and these are things that cannot be learned from an academic checklist of "things to do in the studio under the following conditions." I offer for your consideration a short list of traits that I feel are characteristic of the directors in this collection:

1. They are all perfectionists.
2. They are all intelligent.
3. They are all talented.
4. They like what they do.

First of all, perfection. The ten directors in this collection are all singular, strong-minded individuals, relentless in their pursuit of perfection. In the same breath, they are sensitive enough to know where to draw the line, alert to the nuances of the studio, the feelings of their actors, the temper of their crew, the exigencies of their budget. None of them is casual about his or her art; all enter the control room much the way a perfectly trained athlete enters the auditorium or a playing field, with skills finely honed, ready to do battle. A director uses all of his talent with as much skill as he can muster, and most of the time he's victorious.

As far as intelligence is concerned, I am not inferring that every director is an intellectual giant. In fact, I have always felt that there is more displaced intelligence in the halls of television than in any other of our cultural institutions. It's commonplace to see smart people doing dumb things. But what I saw functioning in the studios and control rooms that I visited was an amalgam of many things, all of which I feel are a mandatory part of the television director's brain scan: logic, memory, alertness, flexibility, adaptability and, most of all, a dedication to using all those things in pursuit of his studio tasks.

Talent is a subjective thing. More than anything, I have a hunch that it's made up of good critical skills, and I'm not sure where you really learn those. If I have any, and I hope I have, I think I learned them in the household of my parents: in the music we listened to, the plays that we attended, the books that we read, the conversations that went on. I cannot understand how graduate students at a major university, like some that I have taught at, can do a dramatic exercise, a play, without ever having seen one or read one. Needless to say, all the people that I interviewed are inveterate seers, viewers, goers to concerts, theatres, movies—you name it—and are most explicit in their notions about what is good and what is bad in what they have seen. All of them know how they can do it better. They are all extremely talented.

Finally, there is something about the glamour of television that is heady stuff. In my own case—and I have said this many times—over the years, in the hundreds of shows that I have worked, with all their attendant problems, I have never for one moment experienced any regret about the life course I chose. I found this universally true of all the people that I interviewed: they like what they do.

Maybe one or two would have liked to improve on the setting for their talent a bit, but to a person, I discerned great joy in the role they are playing. It's a great business, television, and a fine career for anybody who wants to make the commitment. I have had almost forty years of it—and look forward to the next forty.

☆ _____

Update

As I noted, these interviews were conducted between 1983 and 1988. In this collection, they are presented in the order in which they were recorded. I taped the first two (Browning and Grossman) in New York City during the spring of 1983, the next four (Schaefer, Daniels, Mischer and Bogart) in Hollywood during the summer of 1984, and the final four (Tweedy, Auerbach, Squires and Paul) in the fall of 1988, once again in New York City.

As of May 1, 1989:

KIRK BROWNING's productive career goes on uninterrupted. He recently directed the television version of Sigmund Romberg's *New Moon* for PBS's *Great Performance* series, as well as the *70th Birthday Salute to Leonard Bernstein* that circled the globe by satellite. He continues his relationship with the *Live from Lincoln Center* series, recently directing *Andre Watts' 25th-Anniversary Concert.*

SANDY GROSSMAN remains one of CBS Sports' most valuable assets. His credit will be seen every Sunday throughout the football season on at least one National Football League game. When it is CBS's turn to broadcast the Super Bowl, Sandy will be the director. He was also in the control room during most of the highlight games of the *Countdown to the Final Four,* the 1988 telecast of the NCAA Division I finals in college basketball.

GEORGE SCHAEFER's long career reads like a history of American television and theatre. His Broadway credits, like his Pulitzer Prize–winning production of *The Teahouse of the August Moon,* were only a prelude to his long career in television—ninety-four shows in all, which earned him seventy-six awards at last count. He is currently Associate Dean of the Theatre, Film, and Television

Department at UCLA and, through his own Schaefer/Karpf production company, continues to involve himself in innumerable theatre and television projects.

MARC DANIELS's career was on hold when I spoke to him out on the Coast several weeks ago. At the time, he was recovering from some heart surgery, anxious to be back at work. A call from his wife brought the sad news that Marc had died on April 23. We mourn his loss; he was a good man.

DON MISCHER's schedule never ceases to amaze me. Next month he will produce the American Theatre Wing's Antoinette Perry (Tony) Awards for the third time. He recently finished the highly lauded *Tap Dance in America*, which starred Gregory Hines, on PBS. In writing about the show, *People* magazine said, "If the energy from this hour-long special could be harnessed . . . the world's nuclear power plants could be permanently dismantled."* In January of 1989 he produced the *Presidential Inaugural Gala* which was broadcast live on the CBS network on the eve of the inauguration of George Bush.

PAUL BOGART's career has taken a cinematic turn, his latest ventures being created primarily for the big screen. We recently saw his name on the movie version of Harvey Fierstein's play *Torch Song Trilogy,* which starred Matthew Broderick and Anne Bancroft, as well as Mr. Fierstein. But knowing Paul, I am sure that he will never turn his back on television, no matter what seductions film may offer. I expect to see his credit momentarily on any number of splendid TV projects.

LLOYD TWEEDY is still an important part of IBM's corporate investment in television. Since our interview, he has begun a new venture with the company, helping them start a News Satellite Network for employees, which he will supervise. This network will enable IBM to communicate with its 600,000 employees around the world in any number of configurations—everything from personal messages from the chairman to new product announcements. It sounded terrific—a great opportunity for Lloyd.

LARRY AUERBACH continues his successful run on *One Life to Live,* sharing his time with his administrative duties at the Director's Guild of America. *One Life to Live* seems to be flourishing, with good ratings and large audiences, in spite of the continuing decline in network viewing. My projection of Larry's career has him

---

*John Stark, "Picks and Pans," *People*, March 20, 1989.

doing the same thing at the same stand five years from now. What he does he does exceedingly well, and he's well compensated for it, so why not?

EMILY SQUIRES was at home hard at work on her word processor developing an *After School Special* for the networks on environmental pollution. She also has a screenplay in the works using some of this same material. Her season on *Sesame Street* had ended for the year, and she had decided to keep her off-season busy with things that she wants to do, rather than being a "gun for hire." She continues her involvement with New York Women in Film, and as we said good-bye, she was about to go off to a planning meeting for the next season of *Sesame Street*.

GEORGE PAUL no longer does his daily stint on *Today*. Contrary to his expressed wish to continue to do the show, he recently signed a contract with ABC News, changed networks, and now his credit can be seen on *20/20*, ABC's answer to *60 Minutes*. He also expects to work on the ABC *Viewpoint* specials, which are seen six to eight times a year, offering commentary on issues of importance. If the network knows what they have in camp, I would also expect George to be directing the next round of ABC's continuing political coverage—no one does it better.

I also thank George for the title of this collection. Directing live television as he does most of the time, no one is more aware than George that there is only TAKE ONE.

☆

Selected Bibliography

Anderson, Gary H. *Video Editing and Post Production: A Professional Guide.* 2d ed. White Plains, N.Y.: Knowledge Industry Publications, 1988.

Armer, Alan A. *Directing Television and Film.* Belmont, Calif.: Wadsworth Publishing Co., 1984.

Blumenthal, Howard. *Television Producing and Directing.* New York: Harper & Row, 1987.

Bretz, Rudy. *Techniques of Television Production.* New York: McGraw-Hill TV Series, 1962.

Burroughs, Thomas D., and Wood, Donald N. *Television Production.* 2d ed. Dubuque, Iowa: W. C. Brown Co., 1982.

Clurman, Harold. *On Directing.* New York: Macmillan Publishing Co., 1974.

Edmonds, Robert. *The Sights and Sounds of Cinema and Television.* New York: Columbia University, Teacher's College Press, 1982.

Kennedy, Tom. *Directing the Video Program.* White Plains, N.Y.: Knowledge Industry Publications, 1988.

Kindem, Gorham. *The Moving Image, Production Principles and Practices.* Glenview, Ill.: Scott, Foresman, 1987.

Lewis, Colby. *The TV Director/Interpreter.* New York: Hastings House, 1968.

Marlow, Eugene. *Managing Corporate Media.* White Plains, N.Y.: Knowledge Industry Publications, 1988.

Millerson, Gerald. *The Techniques of Television Production.* 11th ed. London and Boston: Focal Press, 1985.

Stasheff, Edward, and Bretz, Rudy. *The Television Program—Its Direction and Production.* 5th ed. New York: Hill and Wang, 1976.

Wurtzel, Alan. *Television Production.* 2d ed. Dubuque, Iowa: W. C. Brown Co., 1982.

Zettl, Herbert. *Sight, Sound, Motion: Applied Media Aesthetics*. Belmont, Calif.: Wadsworth Publishing Co., 1973.
———. *Television Production Handbook*. 4th ed. Belmont, Calif.: Wadsworth Publishing Co., 1984.

☆

Index

About the Author

JACK KUNEY was a producer, director, and writer in television and radio for more than thirty-five years. He was employed by a wide variety of entities, including NBC and CBS, as well as individual stations and public television. He has been the recipient of many awards, among them five "Emmies," awarded by the Academy of TV Arts and Sciences for excellence in television. A retired Professor of Television and Radio from Brooklyn College, Kuney is currently at work on two books and a play.